TRINITY
GUILDHALL

From Page
to Performance

A Teacher's Companion
to the Trinity Guildhall
Grade and Certificate Syllabuses
in Drama and Speech Subjects
and to Anthology Online

Ken Pickering
Foreword by John Gardyne

TRINITY
COLLEGE LONDON

Trinity Guildhall examinations are offered
by Trinity College London,
the international examinations board

First published 2007 by:

Trinity College London
89 Albert Embankment
London SE1 7TP

T +44 (0)20 7820 6100
F +44 (0)20 7820 6161
E info@trinityguildhall.co.uk
www.trinityguildhall.co.uk

Cover photo: Tas Kyprianou

Printed and bound by Stephen Austin & Sons Ltd, Hertford, UK

Contents

Acknowledgements

The author wishes to acknowledge the contributions
in words, ideas and encouragement made by:
Paul Allain, Frank Barrie, John Binfield,
Helen Capper, John Caputo, Bob Cheeseman,
John Gardyne, Patrice Pavis, Eunice Roberts,
Madhulika Varma and Chris Young.

Foreword

Browse through the poetry or drama sections of just about any bookshop in the world and the shelves will be full of collections, anthologies and selections of monologues and scenes. Many of these are published by examination boards and contain a series of 'set pieces' of progressive levels of 'difficulty' that students must perform at the different grade and diploma levels. So an extract from *Pride and Prejudice* may be defined as a 'Grade 7' piece while *The Lion the Witch and the Wardrobe* is 'Grade 2'.

While it is undeniable that some poems and texts are more complex than others – and that some are more appropriate for younger and less experienced candidates than others – straight-jacketing texts for performance into these unyielding categories on the basis of linguistic and grammatical complexity denies a fundamental tenet of live performance. Material that appears initially to be of the utmost simplicity can demand the most sophisticated skills truly to come alive in performance.

Take, for example, Orlando Gibbons' beautiful and celebrated lyric:

The Silver Swan

The silver swan, who living had no note,
When death approached, unlocked her silent throat,
Leaning her breast against the reedy shore,
Thus sung her first and last, and sung no more.
Farewell all joys; O Death come close mine eyes;
More geese than swans now live, more fools than wise.

A short poem, six lines long, easily understood, about a dying animal. But the poem resonates in different ways for readers of different ages and levels of life experience and on re-reading it reveals itself as an almost unbearably poignant reflection on personal disappointment and human mortality. Hearing this poem read aloud by a young child, someone in middle-age or a performer well into their 70s would be profoundly different experiences, but each equally valid.

It was always a keystone of the philosophy of Trinity College London Drama & Speech examinations that candidates have a completely free choice of material and I am pleased to say that this principle has been retained following amalgamation with Guildhall School of Music & Drama's Examinations Service. However, we do understand that teachers and students, especially those coming to the Trinity Guildhall syllabus for the first time, may appreciate some guidelines and examples of the type of pieces that might be suitable at various levels.

Initially we considered printing our own anthology of pieces, similar to those of other examination boards. However, there would always be the likelihood that – however much we said to the contrary – this would become a 'set text' and we would be drifting away from one of the key principles underpinning our work. We were also uncomfortable with the idea of producing a publication that candidates must buy before undertaking our examinations, by implication limiting their choice and burdening them with additional financial outlay.

We therefore have taken the unprecedented step of publishing an anthology on the internet (**www.anthologyonline.org**). This is a free, downloadable resource that offers students and teachers examples of poetry, prose and drama by writers from all historical periods and from over the world. Anthology Online will be continuously revised and updated. Users are invited to add comments and make suggestions, enter into a dialogue with fellow teachers and students and contribute to the ongoing development of this unique resource.

Pieces are not defined by grade, but arranged into three broad bands – Foundation, Intermediate and Advanced – that reflect the levels of achievement defined in our syllabus: Foundation being Initial and Grades 1-3, Intermediate Grades 4-5 and Advanced Grades 6-8.

This book – written by my esteemed predecessor Professor Ken Pickering – provides teachers with further advice and guidance in working with the Trinity Guildhall syllabuses in Drama & Speech. Although some of this material will also be of use to diploma students, it is primarily aimed at candidates undertaking grade and certificate examinations. Diploma students will find further guidance in the Trinity Guildhall handbook *Preparing for your Diploma*[1].

Written in Ken's inimitable style, and drawing on his decades of experience as a teacher, director, examiner and performer, the book reflects his overwhelming enthusiasm and love for his subject. I am sure that it will become an indispensable companion for teachers worldwide.

John Gardyne
Chief Examiner – Drama & Speech
Trinity Guildhall
www.trinityguildhall.co.uk

[1] see Sources and resources

1. First impressions

1. First impressions

You have almost certainly bought this book because you are involved in preparing your students or yourself for Trinity Guildhall examinations in Drama & Speech. This can be a lonely process and, quite understandably, you are seeking guidance and reassurance, especially in choosing and making use of material from the new Anthology Online **www.anthologyonline.org**

So let's deal straight away with some questions you may have at the outset.

Why a new and 'online' anthology?

Since the early years of the last century, the Guildhall School of Music & Drama regularly published an anthology of prose, verse and drama for use in its examinations. Compiled by distinguished teachers and examiners, the Anthology established itself as a major resource, not only for examinations but for the subject as a whole. Its appearance was eagerly anticipated and its content hungrily devoured. Since the 1990s Trinity College London has developed a policy of allowing a free choice of material and encouraged teachers to make the search for such material part of the creative process. Anthology Online represents both traditions: pieces are suggested as suitable for various grades but they are not prescribed and are included as examples rather than 'set pieces'. However, at every level of modern education, there is increasing use of what has become known as 'e-learning' and Trinity Guildhall intends to remain in the vanguard of provision for its teachers and candidates. Accordingly, it was decided to make the Anthology available on the internet to facilitate the constant updating and accessibility of material. An important added dimension is the recognition of the many countries in which Trinity Guildhall examinations are offered and the multi-cultural societies in which many of us live. Although all the pieces are in English, some translated from other languages, the general content is by no means 'euro-centric'.

Why the constant use of the word 'performance'?

Our use of the word 'performance' in the syllabus and this book has already caused some teachers to panic. Quite understandably, they argue that they are not necessarily training performers in the vocational sense and that the skills students develop through their classes are not those required by professional actors.

There are three perfectly good reasons why we use the word 'performance' so constantly:

- *Every time a person makes an oral and/or visual presentation to someone else it constitutes a **performance**.* So it follows that what happens in an examination is a performance and **that is the skill being assessed.**

- *Every item presented in an examination must be capable of being performed in another situation for which it is designed.* For example, a play extract must be capable of 'working' as part of a full production of the play in a theatre and a talk must be able to be given to a target audience. **There is no such thing as an 'exam room performance'.**

- *The idea of 'performance' and 'performance studies' is now an accepted and important part of work in higher (university level) education and we have a duty to acknowledge this development in our subject area.* We have already seen that whenever someone presents any poem or story to someone else a **performance** takes place. There is a growing recognition that there are many kinds of 'performance', ranging from a street procession to grand opera, or from a musical recital to someone relating a personal narrative to a friend. This extraordinary human phenomenon has caught the attention of anthropologists as well as that of theatre scholars and a great deal of fascinating work in 'performance studies' has emanated from New York in the last 20 years or so, particularly influenced by Richard Schechner. If you are interested in furthering your study in this area you should consult some of the books recommended in the 'Sources and resources' section at the end of this book.

It is significant that many recent appointments in colleges and universities use the expression 'Theatre [or Drama] and Performance', and this, of course, also reflects the growing realisation that the boundaries of various kinds of performance, such as drama, dance or mime, are very indeterminate.

Why the emphasis on storytelling?

Because storytelling is the foundation of all oral and physical performance. It is almost certainly their earliest form. Whether it is a highly personal story, as in a lyric poem, or a complex and elaborate narrative told through classical ballet, the telling of a story seems to be a fundamental human activity. Very often, storytelling leads to **enactment** and that is the origin of drama and theatre in a variety of cultures.

Because stories and especially myths are humanity's attempt to make sense of the universe. Stories can bridge cultural divides yet reflect a particular culture. Think how many myths try to explain the Creation. Such stories are the products of the **imagination**, which is the single most important aspect of our practice. We have all experienced young children who create a whole fictitious world of characters: that ability must feed into our work.

Because stories demand that an audience is engaged and in the telling and listening we experience the satisfaction of performance and interaction. Teachers and examiners always long for students to have 'something they want to tell us' and hope to experience that sense of vital energy we first learn as we gather round to hear a story or sit and listen to it told by a loved-one.

Some Drama and Speech students have gained employment as story-tellers in libraries and shopping malls, or included story-telling in their work as nursery assistants or joined theatre companies that tour stories to rural communities. Fortunately there has been a considerable recent upsurge in the rediscovery of the power of stories from many different traditions and some of these are reflected in Anthology Online. Story telling has been shown to enhance language development and emotional security so, if our students become parents or relations of younger people, they are passing on a priceless legacy.

Why the three levels: Foundation, Intermediate and Advanced?

Because Trinity Guildhall's Head Office is based in London and is therefore subject to UK regulation.

As part of its commitment to assure the quality and validity of all qualifications, the UK government established the Qualifications and Curriculum Authority (QCA) in England and similar authorities in Wales and Northern Ireland. After a considerable academic review process and negotiations with awarding bodies in the field of Speech and Drama, the QCA accredited qualifications in this area in the National Qualifications Framework (NQF). This was a very important and significant move because it represented the first official government recognition of the graded examinations system in Speech and Drama. Trinity Guildhall examinations in Drama & Speech (and related subjects) are now accredited by the QCA and can also play a significant role in university entrance. As part of that accreditation process, the various awarding bodies agreed to the positioning of their grades within the established levels for *all* subjects and hence it was agreed that Grades 1-3 would be Foundation level qualifications, Grades 4 and 5 Intermediate level and Grades 6-8 Advanced level. Initial falls just outside the Foundation level, but for the purposes of Anthology Online we have included it there.

There are three particular benefits to keep in mind as you explore and decide how to use Anthology Online:

- *Grades are not defined by their 'set pieces'.* Awarding bodies have been challenged to rethink the nature of syllabuses: they are **not** a series of tasks but a framework for learning and teaching. A grade is defined by the knowledge, skills and understanding demanded and the whole concept of graded examinations assumes the idea of **progressive mastery**. It is, therefore, rather misleading to think of a certain poem as a 'Grade 4 piece' for example. The various works used for examination are means of enabling candidates to achieve the level of skill and understanding required at each grade. It may be perfectly appropriate for one candidate to use a piece at Grade 4 and for another to use it at Grade 5 provided that the 'learning outcomes' are respected.

- *Accreditation means that there are consistent standards across the awarding bodies.* Chief Examiners from the various accredited awarding bodies in Drama and Speech meet regularly to ensure comparability in standards. We are glad that you have chosen to use the Trinity Guildhall syllabus but we constantly remember that you have a choice.

- *Graded examinations are now recognised in some countries as entry qualifications for higher (university level) education.* By being part of a nationally recognised collection of qualifications, graded examinations in our subject are seen as being as valuable as qualifications in a whole variety of other subjects. This belated recognition of the value of what so many teachers and educationalists (and Chief Examiners!) have been striving for is to be welcomed and helps us to see our subject firmly established and properly funded within the school or college curriculum.

Speech and Drama or Drama and Speech? What kind of teacher are you?

If you were asked to describe yourself in terms of your subject, how would you respond? Would you call yourself a 'Speech and Drama' teacher or a 'Drama teacher' or, perhaps, a 'Speech teacher'? You may, of course, subscribe to none of these and prefer to be called a 'Communications Arts teacher', an 'English teacher' or a 'Performing Arts teacher', or you may have started looking at a syllabus because you primarily think of yourself as a 'Dance teacher' or 'Singing teacher'. It is important to be honest about how you see yourself because **that may well determine your approach to the syllabus and to the examples contained in Anthology Online**.

Traditionally, by far the largest group of teachers entering candidates for graded examinations have thought of themselves as teachers of 'Speech and Drama'. This hybrid subject is the successor of what was called 'Elocution and Deportment' in the 18th and 19th centuries and 'Speech Training and Dramatic Art' in the early 20th century. Teachers of this subject have tended to acquire their qualifications through the same awarding bodies that offer graded examinations and have predominantly, although by no means exclusively, worked in the private sector of education. Throughout its distinguished history, this subject has constantly re-invented itself in order to reject the perceived artificiality of previous generations and has frequently struggled to achieve a balance between its two major elements. One of the major problems in that respect has been that the subject has been much influenced by the very extensive and growing understanding of the operation of the human voice. Speech and Drama teachers, as we have come to know them, have often been expected to offer a very wide range of knowledge and skills: these have included an extensive outline knowledge of literature, theatre and drama; performance skills in the presentation of poetry, prose and drama; an ability to correct speech faults; the competence to teach various age-groups of students and the skill to direct a play or understand concepts such as 'period movement'. Such teachers are likely to be drawn to graded examinations entitled 'Speech and Drama'.

But the picture has changed enormously in fairly recent years. Since the late 1940s, with the particular influence of the seminal figure Peter Slade, a very different tradition of play and improvisation-based Child Drama has emerged. Predominantly used in classroom situations within all kinds of schools, this form of drama became to be understood and valued as a means of child development and learning. Educational Drama (as it came to be known) spawned a different kind of teacher; less likely to be concerned with correct speech but more likely to use the understood elements of theatre and drama as a tool for social learning or even for therapy. Like Speech and Drama, what we might broadly term Educational Drama produced a large amount of supporting literature.

Yet another factor has impacted on the kind of examinations that any awarding body might offer and that has been the steady growth of enthusiasm for the Performing Arts as a school, college, or part-time stage school subject. The universal popularity of Musical Theatre together with the rapid development of technology has meant that, for an increasing majority of young people, the experience of 'theatre' or even of 'literature' is through very accessible mechanical and/or electronic media. Youth theatres and similar groups see the natural outcome of their work to be some kind of production or 'show' and, like classroom teachers in schools, may be unlikely to think in terms of examinations for individuals as a way of marking the progress of their students. However, teachers in these situations are now turning to awarding bodies to reward their students' achievements in a way that is appropriate to *their* way of working. **Our syllabus and Anthology Online cater for all of these diverse approaches and traditions.**

When we came to define the name of our general subject area in a collective title for our syllabus we rejected 'Speech & Drama' because that represented a particular tradition and a particular, although still deservedly popular, strand within our syllabus. We felt therefore that **Drama & Speech** was a more accurate representation of the various aspects of the syllabus, that could, for example, include Musical Theatre and Performance Arts which both envisage a type of 'Drama' in the broadest sense of the word. However, we were also aware that some teachers were far more interested in developing communication skills outside the sphere of 'Performance' and so have collected together another strand of examinations under the general heading of 'Communication Skills'. These are currently only marginally represented in Anthology Online, although some pieces may well be suitable in that context.

Under the general heading of 'Acting and Speaking' come all the examinations that, in some form, either employ a written text as a starting point or culminate in the devising of a text. We shall consider that distinction in our next section but, for the moment, it is important for you to notice that we have included examinations that have an emphasis on acting, others with an emphasis on speaking and some that envisage a balance. **The examples in Anthology Online are designed to cater for all these needs.**

In your teaching you are probably going to be more comfortable in one area than another but it is vital that you realise where you are coming from and aim for a **balance** in your work. For example, all examiners have experienced performances in which the dialogue of a devised play has been virtually inaudible or performances where the candidates have been so conscious of trying to produce a beautiful sound that the meaning of their piece has been swamped.

Neither of these situations is acceptable. In addition, far too many candidates 'speak' Shakespeare without acting and far too many 'act' without any idea of the technical requirements and discipline the language and verse forms demand.

Anthology Online not only provides examples of suitable material for Acting and Speaking for individuals, it also provides material for pairs and groups and there are pieces that may be used as the basis for improvised and devised work. We must now turn our attention to the fact that any anthology, online or otherwise, is a collection of **texts** and consider the consequences.

Text and context

The collection of prose, poems and drama that we have assembled is both varied and fascinating. Post-modernist students of Performance Studies tend to use the word 'text' to define the entire collection of performance features that may emerge in rehearsal of what they like to call 'the work'. So, for them, a 'text' might include the physical movement, the sequence of lighting or sounds, or the action that derives from the original work. Companies such as Theatre de Complicite, The Wooster Group and Mamo Mines frequently create works that reject the idea that that the original 'text' is in any way fixed or sacred, and use it merely as a starting point for their own exploration and discovery. Some playwrights such as Arthur Miller have violently objected to this treatment of their plays. For further discussion of this concept of 'text' see the chapter entitled Teachers' Terms and Tools.

We are encouraging a more conservative view of the **text** as the most important basis of a performance but we acknowledge that imaginative use of a text is also a highly desirable feature. We would certainly not advocate changes to the texts of poems, plays, novels or other established works of prose but some pieces may well be re-worked into something more appropriate to the level of achievement or form the starting point for

other 'texts'. We look at examples of these possibilities as we study the contents of Anthology Online more closely.

If you survey the total contents of the Anthology you will notice several key points and, although they may seem obvious, it is important to note some of these:

The texts are really of two different kinds – **those that are complete in themselves** and **those that are extracts**. What is the implication of this fact?

Before we attempt to answer this question remember one vital fact concerning the texts. Almost invariably, the candidates who are most successful in Drama & Speech examinations are those who have taken the time and effort to study and master the text fully.

Notice, as you look through Anthology Online, that many of the pieces are **relatively short**. Short pieces are not necessarily an easy option. On the contrary, you will find that, if you undertake the kind of preparation and close attention to the text we recommend, some short pieces are very demanding and capable of the most subtle interpretation.

You may also note that a considerable number of the pieces are **translations**, especially in the drama section where we have included important and influential pieces from a number of non-English sources. There are also translations of poems and historic prose texts. You will find that some ancient texts have been updated with modern spelling and language. Wherever a piece is not in its original form you should examine it very carefully and **consider if the translation we have provided is the best for your needs.** You may well find that the translation we have used (e.g. for Greek Drama) is only one of many available and that you are able to discover a new and more appropriate translation. Please use our collection as a starting point rather than as a definitive version, or, if you have the skill, make your own translation!

Let's now return to the two questions we posed earlier regarding whole pieces and extracts. Make sure that you have decided

Let me illustrate the absolutely vital importance of studying and mastering the text fully, with a personal anecdote:

Some years ago I was asked to direct a major production in which the lead role was to be played by the fine actor Peter Barkworth (whose books on acting still seem to me to be the best and most accessible guides to the art form)[1]. A few days after he had received the script I arranged to spend a morning with him discussing possible approaches to his part. I was astonished to be offered a choice of at least ten ways of speaking the opening two lines of the play! Clearly, Peter had explored every possible shade of meaning, every word, punctuation mark, nuance of the language and every conceivable use of phrasing, pause, inflection, stress, emphasis and pace. He had examined the text with scrupulous care and could relate those opening two lines to everything that followed in the play. With his skill the entire text came alive and compelled you to listen to it. The most complex ideas were made simple, the most profound emotions tangible. Of course, I am talking about a great professional actor and a highly complex and demanding script but even the most junior candidates will benefit enormously if you encourage them to apply a similarly analytical approach to the pieces they are preparing. If they are unable to do so, you may have chosen the wrong piece or the wrong grade.

piece was written, what form it takes and what its subject is: in fact, we have already begun to set the piece in some **context**. That will tell us what else we need to know in order to make sense of the piece.

For example: because of the various continents and countries involved in Trinity Guildhall examinations we decided to include some pieces about cricket. While these are entire in themselves they would almost certainly be completely incomprehensible without some additional contextual understanding. For example, you would not know how to speak the Foundation level poem *Whacks and Wickets* by Annette Kosseris effectively unless you understood the meaning of the word 'wicket'. That apparently simple word alone contains two and possibly three meanings.

You can extend this to any item of literature or drama you may encounter: a sonnet by Shakespeare will only make sense if you have some concepts of Renaissance ideas of mutability and the use of emblematic language, and so on. At this point you should note that the detailed preparation required by even the most apparently simple piece might influence the amount of time spent over each grade. Our experience at Trinity Guildhall is that candidates and their teachers are sometimes in far too great a hurry to move from one grade to the next. The golden rule is **take your time and prepare thoroughly**.

In a later chapter you will find a **checklist for preparation** but for the moment we must continue our consideration of **context** and turn to pieces that are extracts from longer works. You may notice that we also invite you to make your own selection from the material we have supplied; **the extracts we have provided do not have to be used in their entirety**.

into which category the piece you are considering falls. If the piece is entire you have the advantage of being able to see the writer's total form, shape and design. The opening, the middle and the ending will be as the writer intended for a complete experience. However short the piece, the clues to its meaning lie almost exclusively in the text and we shall be looking at the process whereby we seek out those meanings in much greater detail at a later stage. At the first impression stage we can note when the

Generally, it is much more difficult to speak an extract from a poem. It is sometimes possible to perform part of very long narrative poems such as *Paradise Lost* or *In Memoriam* but, normally, a poem is already very intense, detailed and narrowly focused and these qualities are lost if we do not

[1] see Sources and resources

present the entire piece. Poems also have a very precise form, often built around metre, rhythm and rhyme and it is as difficult to make a shorter version of a poem as it is a song or piece of instrumental music. It may well be possible to take part of a poem and use it as a text for another genre of performance. Performance Arts examinations offer an opportunity to devise new pieces of theatre that integrate fragments of text, music, dance, media, design and so on and you should not hesitate to use the material we have provided in this way. Examiners at a recent standardisation conference were held spellbound by a video of a solo performance from South Africa that used intense physical action, effective costume and some text from T S Eliot to explore the problem of AIDS, and, in that sense, it is entirely possible to take a piece 'out of context' to create new meanings.

Many of the prose passages and pieces of drama in Anthology Online are taken from longer works. In both cases there are additional contextual considerations: whereabouts in the entire work does this piece come? Who is speaking and what do we know about them already? Where are they, who are they and what is happening to them? These are just some of the questions that we must ask. A much fuller consideration of such factors will appear in our **checklist for preparation of examination pieces** in a later chapter. By including many extracts in our collection we are attempting, among other things, to whet your appetite for the entire work – and indeed other works by the same writer. We have attempted to give as much contextual information as is needed to get you started but we would hope that, wherever possible, you and your students will read the **complete text**.

Drama is particularly built around an understanding of context. Characters, like ourselves, are partially the product of previous experience and, unless we understand this, any performance of a 'character' will be, at best, two-dimensional. We also need to establish the setting in time and place and have some comprehension of

the type of theatre and performance for which the play was originally written. However, we need to be equally aware that the process by which a text becomes a performance involves an awareness of cultural and aesthetic expectations and of modern practice. Styles of acting and speaking are constantly changing and, unless we saturate ourselves in the life of drama and theatre today, we are likely to produce an outmoded and incongruous performance. Further suggestions for the preparation of drama appears in our **checklist**.

*The most important point for teachers and students to appreciate is that **all the pieces included in Anthology Online existed previously in another context**.* They were not written for, or intended for use in examinations and we have an absolute duty to discover and understand their original context before we try to use them in the exam room. There is, of course, a problem when using books of monologues, duologues or, indeed, some of the examples in Anthology Online itself when it comes to extracts from plays or prose works. Even though we have given information about the original publication of each piece, it may be difficult for you to obtain the entire original work or even for you to track it down. At Trinity Guildhall we welcome enquiries about pieces if you have difficulty in consulting the original but, if it does prove impossible, ask your student to be absolutely honest in the examination and tell the examiner that it has not been possible to see the original work in its entirety. You may have to be a little inventive in your approach if, for example, you wish to use a dramatisation of a novel. In this case, you may have to look at the original novel itself rather than be able to see the entire dramatisation because that script is likely to still be in the hands of the theatre company that commissioned it.

You will notice in the syllabus that we no longer stipulate that the play from which an extract is taken is a **published play**. There are a number of reasons for this; firstly, the advent of 'desktop publishing' has created an entirely new concept of publishing and almost anyone who has written a play can 'publish' it. Secondly, we are anxious to encourage the use of new and original work and, thirdly, there is often a very long time gap between the first performance of a play and its eventual publication (as there clearly was with Shakespeare's plays) and we do not wish to deprive candidates of the opportunity of using such material simply because it has not been 'published'. There are several pieces in Anthology Online that fall into this category.

The contextual information we have supplied ought to be sufficient to get you started on the process of finding out more about the various works and remember not to confuse **useful insights into the text** with **rather useless details about the lives of the writers!** We shall be exploring the idea of what is useful in a later chapter.

What about English Literature?

Before you read this short section you may wish to read – and enjoy – *The Stranglehold of English Lit.* by Felix Mnthali, a contemporary poet from Malawi (Advanced Poetry section). You may be surprised that we would want to include this defiant rejection of the monster of English Literature but let's get it clear from the outset, Trinity Guildhall examinations in Drama & Speech are not, nor ever have been, examinations in literature. It is perfectly true that many teachers have used them as a complement to studies in English Literature and may well have used some of the same material. However, our examinations are essentially designed to assess performance skills and the greatest of these skills is the ability to **respond vocally and physically to the quality and substance of a text**.

As we have seen, a very thorough understanding of the material being presented is essential and that may include placing the work in the context of its position in English Literature **but** one of the intentions of producing Anthology Online is to introduce candidates to world literature written or translated into English. The growing interest in what has become known as world music is surely one of the healthiest and most welcome artistic movements of our age and at Trinity Guildhall we would like to take a lead in promoting an interest in world literature. This may take us back to explore ancient, neglected texts as well as promoting the work of new writers from around the world.

As you browse through Anthology Online you will find many examples of such works. There are still 'classics' of English literature but a great number of the pieces are by living and, quite often, little-known writers. There are works by very young writers and some that are being published for the first time. We are anxious that you realise that embarking on work with Trinity Guildhall is not an introduction to membership of the 'Dead Poets' Society': many of the pieces are by living authors who share a world with the young people who will speak their words and act their plays.

The lack of information about the lives of some of the writers may, in fact, focus the mind on what really matters: *what are this writer's concerns?* Again, we have provided sufficient information to establish a context and we will be offering further advice on what is expected in terms of knowledge and understanding when presenting a play, poem or passage of prose for examination.

The exception to the varied, international fare in Anthology Online is in the Advanced Drama section where we have provided material that meets the demands of the syllabus in terms of historic progression. It is an inescapable fact that since Christopher Marlowe and his contemporaries (including Shakespeare) established London as the most prolific and progressive centre of drama in English, English-speaking theatre around the world has taken its lead from what has happened in Britain and, more recently, the USA. We make no apologies for including some masterpieces from the London stage and believe that competence in performing such material is vital for anyone interested in acting. Nevertheless, we hope that all teachers and students will constantly visit theatres in their own country and experience at first hand the incredible richness of new writing now available.

The last thing we wish to suggest is that we do not want candidates to experience the thrill of engaging with great writing, but it is far more important that they develop the skills required to make writing leap off the page and that the material they explore has some relevance to their lives.

How to use the rest of this book

Our intention is that this is a genuine 'handbook' that you keep to hand whenever and wherever you are working. It is also a 'companion' that we hope will become part of your working methods and approach. For this reason, the book is written in short, digestible sections that you may wish to re-visit frequently, and we have made use of lists and checklists to simplify the presentation and use of information.

In subsequent chapters there will be discussion of the process of making good and suitable choices of material together with suggestions for preparing such material for examinations. We shall explore the elements of our subject, consider detailed examples of ways of working and think about the use and relevance of what has become known as 'theory'. We shall then consider the role and demands of improvisation and mime before turning to a reference section in which many of the terms and concepts of Drama and Speech are explored. This is followed by an important case-study of approaches to Shakespeare and a list of sources. You should note that, at various stages, there are suggestions for further reading. The details of the books concerned will appear in the 'Sources and resources' section but you should also frequently consult publishers' catalogues and the reviews sections of relevant journals for details of the most recent publications. If you or your students

ever experience difficulties in studying please refer to the excellent website www.skills4study.com

So, now let's consider some of the issues of making your choice of material.

2. Making your choice

2. Making your choice

Making the best possible choice of material for an examination is one of the keys to success for any candidate. Many teachers will feel so confident that they can do this from their knowledge of the syllabus and of their students that they will need little help. Others may be anxious or tentative because they sense changes in expectations or because they lack experience. Whoever you are, it is worth thinking about the variables that make up the criteria for choice.

A piece for examination must:

- be suitable for the age and experience of the candidate
- be appropriate to the candidate's culture, interests and abilities
- enable the candidate to demonstrate his or her skills
- fulfil the requirements of the learning outcomes for the level of examination
- fulfil the detailed syllabus requirements of the particular grade
- be worth 'living with' for several months
- be entirely within the candidate's level of understanding
- where appropriate, form part of a varied and interesting programme of performances
- fit within the timing requirements for the particular grade. It is irresponsible and unhelpful to equip candidates with pieces that over-run the time allocation.

A note about gender

It was tempting to add to the list above 'suitable for the candidate's gender' but that is a complex issue. In a great deal of world drama there are examples of 'cross-gender' casting. Ancient forms of theatre performance have often employed elaborate costumes and acting styles to enable men and boys to play women's roles and there have been plenty of examples of women taking men's roles. Large territories of drama open up if

you are not confined to casting with gender. However, where the 'voice' behind a poem or prose passage is clearly male or female it may be perverse to go against this and the only question that must remain is '**does this piece enable the candidate to satisfy all the other requirements listed above?'**.

The most common problem

Without any shadow of doubt, **the most frequent problem examiners experience in running grade examinations is that the choice of material is beyond the candidate's comprehension and experience.**

An overview of the choices required in Speech and Drama examinations

It is helpful if we now summarise the choices of material you will have to make for our most popular syllabus strand: Speech and Drama (solo). We are **not** for the moment considering choices relating to mime or improvisation as we shall be dealing with these separately in chapter 5.

You should be able to refer back to the checklist opposite throughout your use of this book.

As you study this list you will see clearly demonstrated the concept of **progressive mastery** on which the graded examination system is based. In particular, note the introduction of **sight reading** as an option at Intermediate (Grade 4) level, the **considerable increase in demand** at Advanced level (Grade 6 and higher) and the possible involvement of **another actor** from Grade 7 onwards. It is only at Advanced level that there is any mention of the idea of finding **contrasting** pieces.

Before we explore the implications of the syllabus for making choices of material we also need to think about the knowledge and understanding that candidates are asked to demonstrate as they progress through the grades – there is a checklist on page 20.

Checklist of choices of material for Speech and Drama (solo) examinations:

Initial
- An original, traditional or folk story
- A poem

Grade 1
- A prose passage or short extract from a play
- A poem

Grade 2
- A prose passage or play extract
- A poem
- A book (from which the prose passage, play extract or poem may be taken)

Grade 3
- A prose passage or play extract
- A poem
- A book (from which the prose passage, play extract or poem may be taken)

Grade 4
- A prose passage or play extract
- A poem

Grade 5
- A prose passage or play extract
- A poem

Grade 6
- An extract from a play written in or after 1956
- A narrative poem (whole or part)
- A passage of narrative prose (contrasting in mood to the above)

Grade 7
- A play extract from the 16th or 17th century
- A lyric poem or lyric verse passage
- A contrasting prose passage

Grade 8
- A play extract by a contemporary writer
- A contrasting play extract
- A lyric poem or lyrical verse passage
- A narrative poem or passage of narrative prose

Checklist of knowledge and understanding required through the grades in Speech and Drama (solo) examinations:

Initial and Grades 1 and 2

■ *General conversation about the pieces.* This may take many forms but is intended to explore the candidate's understanding of, and feeling for, the pieces. Examiners may encourage candidates to expand on any relevant topic that arises in a very informal and non-threatening way.

Grade 3

■ *An understanding of the use of **pausing and emphasis***. Note that we introduce the use of the rather more formal term 'discussion' to describe what happens here, together with a requirement that candidates **demonstrate** their understanding. This means that they must be able to point to the use they have made of **pausing and emphasis** in their chosen pieces.

Grade 4

■ *An understanding of the pieces and their **context**. The use of **phrasing and pace in the performance***. Note that this is the first time that the word **context** is used. We are now at Intermediate level and the demands are that much more sophisticated. This level demands a greater sense of enquiry into the background and source of the pieces chosen.

Grade 5

■ *An understanding of the pieces and their context together with an ability to demonstrate the use of **inflection and intonation** in the **performance***. Further information on all these technical terms are to be found in the Trinity Guildhall handbook ***Speech and Drama***[1].

Grade 6

■ *With this movement into Advanced level the syllabus asks for some knowledge of the **author's output** together with the meaning and context of the pieces and of **physical aspects of performance** including **relaxation and breathing***. Again, you will notice a considerable increase in the levels of knowledge and understanding demanded and, although the candidates are a long way from diploma level, you may well find it helpful to consult the Trinity Guildhall handbook ***Preparing for your Diploma in Drama and Speech***[2] to explore recent ideas on physical performance.

Grade 7

■ *An understanding of the meaning and context of the pieces together with a particular appreciation of the writers' use of **language** and the use of **resonance** and **articulation** in the performance*. Note that this is the first time that candidates are asked specific questions about the use of **language** and this implies very thorough consideration of that element of the material.

Grade 8

■ *At this grade examiners are looking for an **integrated understanding** of the factors that impact upon a performance: this will range from the nature of the pieces themselves to the use of performance techniques that have been discussed at previous grades*. There is also an opportunity for candidates to demonstrate their appreciation of and enthusiasm for a particular genre or author. By this grade, candidates should be demonstrating a sense of **ownership** of their performances and far less of a teacher's input. All teachers should remember the words from a poem by C Day Lewis: **love is proved in the letting go!**

[1 & 2] see Sources and resources

So what have the 'theoretical' requirements at each grade got to do with the choices of material?

Everything! We shall devote an entire chapter to 'theory' (as it is sometimes called) but, unless we can apply this body of knowledge and understanding to our practical work it is *totally useless*. Candidates must be able to see and demonstrate the relevance of what they have learned and *this means being able to do this in the pieces they have chosen*.

And what's the difference between a 'conversation' and a 'discussion'?

This question is sometimes asked by anxious teachers who feel that, somehow, the syllabus is a series of mysterious tricks devised to ensnare them. Nothing could be further from the truth!

We use the term 'conversation' to describe an informal exchange with the examiner. The emphasis will be on simple facts and information: some simply designed to put candidates at ease and some to discover ways of working and levels of understanding.

'Discussion' will involve opinions and even debate as well as exchanges of information and contextual knowledge.

What should I have gained from this overview of the choices and topics in the syllabus?

More than anything else you should have seen that the **syllabus is not a series of tasks**. The syllabus provides a **framework** for **creative learning and teaching**. Each grade and level of the syllabus is something to be lingered over and explored thoroughly and at a leisurely pace. You will see in this overview that we not only provide a balance of material in the choices you have to make but also provide enough options for candidates to play to their strengths. There is also the

opportunity for candidates to specialise further. If, for instance, a candidate gradually becomes very enthusiastic about acting, they can move into the 'solo acting' strand of the syllabus, or, if they become uncomfortable with the demands of acting, they can move to the 'performing text' strand. That is why these strands of the syllabus are printed alongside each other.

Any overview of the syllabus ought to provide you, as a teacher, with the material you need to plan your approach, your **strategies** and your **learning outcomes**, and these will almost certainly be different for every student or group of students.

You will also notice the enormous amount of **freedom you are given in making your choices**. We hope that this will encourage you to make the selection of material an integral and exciting part of the entire learning process and that you will use this challenge to explore new writing, either with or without the starting points suggested in Anthology Online (**www.anthologyonline.org**).

Let's get down to making a choice

We'll imagine that you are looking for suitable pieces for a candidate for Grade 3 in Speech and Drama. If you glance at the checklist on page 19 you will see that you have to find a poem and either a prose passage or play extract. At first you may decide that you and your student are not sure whether to select prose or drama so your initial effort will go into finding a poem.

Look at the levels of achievement (learning outcomes) for Foundation level in the Trinity Guildhall syllabus.

Remember that Grade 3 is the highest grade in **Foundation level** and that, therefore, there should be a sense of the candidate having comfortably achieved the desired outcomes.

The material chosen will form the basis of the **performance** so look initially at what is printed under that heading:

'Candidates will typically be able to apply their knowledge, understanding and skills to produce a performance which demonstrates understanding and thoughtful interpretation, based on creative engagement with the materials and careful preparation. They will speak from memory, audibly and clearly and mostly accurately, with a free and fluent delivery, a sense of spontaneity, and conscious awareness of audience, sustaining these qualities to the end. Through variations in volume, pace and pitch they will be able to create and convey mood (e.g. humour, fear). Their apt use of body and space will complement their vocal performance.'

Before we go any further you might like to underline what you consider to be the **key ideas** of this passage.

As this is to be one of the major bases for our choice let's dissect the passage. Here are some of the key words and phrases together with some comments on them:

Performance and Audience
These terms are a timely reminder that this is an examination in performance and not in English literature. The examiner is the 'audience' and whatever piece is chosen must be capable of engaging that audience.

Interpretation
At this level a candidate is expected to present something much more than audible print. They need to have pieces well within their emotional and intellectual range to which they can bring their own, distinctive response in performance.

Knowledge
This will include knowledge of the techniques necessary for audibility and clarity, of the content of the pieces and of the use of pausing and emphasis. Technical terms in voice production are not required.

Understanding
A thorough comprehension of the pieces chosen (as a result of careful preparation) and an understanding of the application of various performance skills, including the necessity of engaging an audience.

Skills
*These will include **vocal** skills to ensure audibility and clarity, **performance** skills in the use of pause, emphasis, volume, pace and pitch, **physical** skills to enable the body to be an expressive instrument and an **integration** of all these skills to provide an individual interpretation. Skills in improvisation, storytelling and/or sight reading are also included.*

Spontaneity
*Material must be so well prepared and familiar to the candidate that, in performance, it will appear that the words have been **created afresh** at that moment. Work in improvisation should also appear effortless and fluent.*

Memory
This is also a skill that needs to be developed.

If you consider all these factors you can see that, to some extent, all must be fed in to your act of choice. Ask yourself this question before we think about the material in detail: **Will the pieces I select with my student enable him or her to demonstrate all these skills at an appropriate level?**

Now we turn to what the learning outcomes say about the material expected at Foundation level:

'Performance skills will be demonstrated through material of sufficient length to allow candidates to show their ability to establish and sustain their performance and interpretation. Content will go beyond easily recognisable events and stories so that candidates can begin to explore emotions, moods and atmosphere outside their immediate experience (e.g. from other periods). The language will contain a variety of expressive vocabulary and a range of syntax, offering some opportunity for interpretative choices.'

What do these key words and phrases mean?

Sufficient length
At Grade 3 we allow a maximum of 10 minutes for the first four tasks and these are roughly equal in length. Thus, we are looking for two

performance pieces of about two to two-and-a-half minutes each – although you may of course choose to balance a shorter piece with a longer one.

Establish and sustain performance and interpretation

*This is an extension of the previous point. If a piece is too short a candidate will find it difficult to expand into the work and enable the audience to feel a sense of sharing and of relaxed listening. Very short pieces may also lack the complexity of ideas needed to inspire a thoughtful performance. However, you should think even now why it is that a **sonnet** is so demanding.*

Outside their immediate experience

At first glance, this requirement may seem to contradict the emphasis we have placed on relevance and modern writing in the Anthology: but that is not the case. We believe that young people must be made aware that literature and drama are about their world and that writers are still as active as ever. However, we also want to take them beyond the commonplace and into other sets of ideas, cultures, periods and attitudes. Sometimes this will involve introducing pieces from ancient literature or writing from another country, or it may extend the language with which the candidate is familiar or take them into a world of the imagination. You will find that every piece we have included extends experience in some way.

Can begin

We are obviously not looking for high levels of sophistication here: these are the foundations on which we build at higher grades.

Emotions, moods and atmosphere

The education of the emotions is one of the major aims of our work. It is often through the arts that we can explore beliefs, feelings and moods in their many manifestations and that intangible quality we call 'atmosphere'. When we come to prepare a piece for performance we ask such questions as, 'What is the predominant mood here?' Exploring emotions beyond their immediate experience through writing and imagination will help young people to grow and their skill will become more sophisticated as they learn how to convey these qualities in performance. Pieces rich in emotional content are more likely to provide a stimulating experience.

Expressive vocabulary

*It is precisely for this reason that the syllabus stipulates a range of poetry, prose and drama but a candidate **must** be able to respond to the quality of the language. Initially we would hope that candidates simply enjoy using words and luxuriating in their expressiveness: there may, indeed, be a time when young people's love of the sound of language outruns their comprehension: this is part of the preparation experience. By the time that candidates are ready for examination they should be able to enjoy all the aspects of language: meaning, sound, images and the way that words work with other words.*

Syntax

The ways in which sentences and language are structured affects the complexity of ideas with which we can deal. At one time, teachers were greatly influenced by the work of Baisl Bernstein in the field of language development: he argued that children either use a 'restricted code' or an 'elaborated code' of language depending on how they had assimilated the use of language from their environment, especially their parents. Although few teachers now use this terminology the fact remains that if a child only hears and then uses a very limited and simple vocabulary and sentence structure, they are unlikely to become articulate or be able to handle complex ideas. Choices in Speech and Drama exams should make a genuine contribution to the developing linguistic, negotiating and reasoning skills of the candidates.

Interpretative choices

*To give one example: Colin Thiele's **Hamburgers** in the Foundation Poetry section of Anthology Online provides considerable scope for individual interpretation. The ambiguity of the piece together with the mood in which it might be presented: ironic,* *enthusiastic, rather solemn, for example, give ample scope for an imaginative response from the speaker. The more possible ways there are of using the language and syntax of the poem, the more stimulating is the result. The important attitude for the teacher is that there is **no set way of speaking a poem** provided that its meaning, form and structure are respected.*

A working example

We are continuing to imagine that you are seeking a suitable piece of poetry for a Grade 3 candidate. After taking all the factors we have been examining into consideration and, above all, **knowing your student,** suppose that you decide to introduce him or her to the poem *To a Butterfly* by the English poet William Wordsworth that we have included in the Foundation section of Anthology Online. This poem was written in 1801 when the poet was 21 and is actually one of two poems he wrote with this title. What are the elements of 'Grade threeness' that make this so suitable?

For convenience in our discussion the poem is reproduced here:

To a Butterfly

I've watch'd you now a full half hour,
Self-poised upon that yellow flower:
And, little Butterfly! indeed
I know not if you sleep or feed.
How motionless! – not frozen seas
More motionless! – and then
What joy awaits you, when the breeze
Hath found you out among the trees,
And calls you forth again!

This plot of orchard-ground is ours;
My trees they are, my Sister's flowers,
Here rest your wings when they are weary;
Here lodge as in a sanctuary!
Come often to us, fear no wrong;
Sit near us on this bough!
We'll talk of sunshine and of song,
And summer days, when we were young;
Sweet childish days, that were as long
As twenty days are now.

Our first consideration: is it the right length?

This poem takes no longer than a minute and a half in performance and is well within the time allowed for this grade. If you experiment with speaking it so that it does last 90 seconds, you will find that it yields up many layers of thought that make it substantial and demanding: so, it is not too short. It is, in fact, of sufficient length to enable the candidate to demonstrate skills in the use of pace, pitch, volume, pause and emphasis as well as the physical aspects of vocal performance.

Two ways of seeing: context and 'afterlife'

There are two basic ways of thinking about a piece: its original context and its possible relevance and performance today. What can we usefully say about the poem in these two ways?

In one sense, the poem extends the candidate's 'immediate experience' by being written over 200 years ago and using expressive vocabulary and syntax that may be somewhat, though not spectacularly, unfamiliar. As teachers, we should know that Wordsworth was writing in an intellectual climate when authority and order had been challenged by the events of the French Revolution and in which poets were increasingly turning to Nature as the source of teaching and, even, moral guidance. He was, in fact, part of the Romantic movement that affected many of the arts. At Grade 3 a candidate does not need to understand all that, but **does** need to recognise that sense of careful observation of nature and be aware of the general time when the poem was written.

Equipped with some of the information we have established, we can return to focus on our chosen poem. Here is a piece written in 1801 by a young man of 21 who clearly had a sister with whom he shares a love of woods and flowers. Specifically, they 'own' an orchard (can your student envisage what is almost certainly an apple orchard?) and the poet particularly likes the trees, and his sister,

Time: a brief but important digression.

Before we continue our previous line of thinking I want to consider the whole issue of time and context for young people. Recently, a colleague who teaches drama and literature at a university was lamenting to me how little her students knew or understood about their own history. This makes the setting of any piece of literature into its original context extremely difficult: it is, of course, even more difficult if the original context was not in the country where the student is now living. Why, on earth, for example, should candidates from Canada, South Africa, Sri Lanka, India, Ireland, Australia, Hong Kong, Malta and New Zealand be particularly interested in what was happening in the Lake District in England 200 years ago? Candidates from these and other countries have very rich histories of their own to explore, histories that have produced fine writing of the kind included in Anthology Online. However, if candidates and their teachers select pieces because they genuinely like and admire them, it is necessary to understand something of their origin.

I always find that the best way to establish time is to relate it to the known and then move to the unknown. Which member of your family was alive when this piece was written? Was the building in which you are having your lessons standing then? If not, which buildings in your neighbourhood were? What was happening in your country when this piece was written? What were the modes of transport? What things that we take for granted now were not available then? What were people wearing? At a more sophisticated level, who was in government? All these questions can help establish something about the context of a piece of literature and are more important than biographical details of the author. At higher levels we ask about the author's other work but, at Foundation level, this is not necessary knowledge. It *is*, however, significant to know *when* and *where* (in terms of country at least) the author was living and at *what stage in life* the author wrote the chosen piece.

the flowers. Given that this is the case is it not unexpected that the poet gives such attention to a butterfly?

But what else tells us that this poem was not written last year? Certainly expressions like 'a full half hour', 'I know not' or 'calls you forth' are somewhat archaic, as is the use of 'hath'. The candidate is being extended and enriched here but **must** be able to provide a precise meaning of each of these expressions **in their own words**. For example, you might ask your student how **they** would say 'I've watch'd you now a full half hour' to convey exactly the same meaning and, of course, explain why 'watch'd' and not 'watched'!

You will also want to give special consideration of the line 'Here lodge as in a sanctuary': a line dense with mood, expressiveness, atmosphere and emotion that could be

the focus of discussion and attention for a prolonged period. The suggestion that you might lavish so much attention to a single line **may** come as a surprise, but it is only by such close attention that you can achieve the learning outcomes for the top of the Foundation level and provide your students with the basis for interpretation. You may be very glad that you have chosen a short poem.

So we have a poem written by a 21-year-old in 1801: a time when things were certainly more leisurely for some and when people were not texting each other in a kind of truncated language. Even at the age of 21, this writer is looking back to a period in his life when time seemed to move more slowly; a nostalgia for the past, perhaps, that is not uncommon in some circles today. Thus, we can place this poem both in its wider context and in the context of the writer's experience.

Another way of seeing

This leads us to think about the poem as being suitable for speaking today – to give it what the theatre director Jonathan Miller calls 'an afterlife'. To what extent is it within the grasp of a modern student who is likely to be quite young?

Firstly, let's return to the idea of the orchard. Even if your student can envisage an orchard it is possible that they have not been in one, that there are no such things in their part of the world and that it is highly unlikely that they could claim to own one.

It may well be that Wordsworth did not actually imply legal ownership of an orchard by the words 'this plot ... is ours'; he may simply be implying emotional ownership in the same way that we might say 'these mountains are mine', but, even so, this could be an experience well outside that of a modern student. However, through **imagination** (a quality on which Wordsworth had a great deal to say elsewhere) it is possible to share that experience. What matters now is that, through performance, the experience is created afresh for a modern audience and the poem has something significant to say to a contemporary performer. The focus may now be on the fact that there are still butterflies and other beautiful living things to be observed. They are just as capable of filling us with wonder now as they were 200 years ago and the same stillness and care are needed in order to observe and appreciate them. Modern people might well talk to butterflies as they settle on a finger in very much the same spirit as Wordsworth. If that first-hand experience is not possible for a student in their immediate environment, it may be possible to seek it out in a zoo or butterfly farm, through books, film, video or nature programmes on TV.

The idea of the fragility of the butterfly and the wish to provide it with sanctuary and protection, the concept of well-being instilled by watching it, the way that it evokes music and sunshine; all these ideas are there for the modern performer to explore.

In performance, it would be difficult to find a better example of the need to employ pause and emphasis – think of the first line:

'I've watch'd you now a full half-hour,'

In order to convey the **mood** and **situation** of this line we need a very slow **pace** but we must also select the pauses and emphasis to aid our **interpretation**: and, yes, **we do have a choice.**

We might speak the first line like this:

'I've [*tiny pause*] watch'd you [*tiny pause*] now [*pause*] a full [*tiny pause*] half-hour, [*long pause*]'

Or we might speak it like this:

'I've watch'd you now [*long pause*] [*much slower*] a full [*pause*] half [*pause*] hour'

Then we might add:

'I've **watch'd** you now a full **half-hour**'

or:

'I've watch'd you **now** a full **half-hour**'

or even:

'**I've** watch'd you now a full half-**hour**'.

Or think of the line:

'Sit near us on the bough'.

Where would you place the pauses and emphasis and how would you help your student to demonstrate this in discussion? Would you recommend:

'**Sit** [*pause*] near us [*pause*] **on** the bough'

or:

Sit **near** us [*pause*] on the bough'

or:

'Sit near **us** [*pause*] on the **bough**'

or:

'Sit **near** us on the **bough** [*long pause*]'?

I hope this illustrates the multitude of interpretative choices provided by this short poem and the comparative ease with which we can make the required learning at any grade relevant to the performance.

After all that, you may well be thinking that we have made the process of selecting pieces for performance incredibly complicated and that it would have been far easier had we done that for you. But you should be assured that once you have followed through the suggestions a few times they will become almost second nature to you and they will both enrich your teaching and enable you to establish an even more positive relationship with your students.

As has been noted already, Trinity Guildhall is committed to students having a completely free choice of material. We feel that an awarding body, based in London, should not dictate to teachers and students all over the world the precise nature of the material they should be reading and performing – especially when you consider that such work must become part of a student's emotional and intellectual experience before he or she can consider transforming it into a performance.

Selecting drama

Yoga teachers sometimes say: '**feel** what you are doing and **why** you are doing it; **savour** what's happening to you.' Precisely the same could be said of the best experiences of performing drama.

The late and greatly missed teacher, writer and examiner, Dr Paul Ranger, often used to speak of 'exam room drama': a phenomenon that had no meaning or purpose outside the examination situation and appeared to bear no relation to anything you might see in a theatre or film. Indeed, 'exam room drama' is so isolated from reality that artificiality seems to be its major characteristic.

Drama is not simply another branch of Speaking or of English Literature. It may involve a written text but the speaking of words is not its root. Whereas you may ask if a poem or piece of prose is within the comprehension and speaking skills of a student, you should be asking **totally different questions** of a piece of drama as it appears on the printed page. Here are some of them:

- As a teacher preparing this student do I have the theatrical experience to direct the performance?
- Can my student see live theatre performances?
- Has he/she ever been in a play and does the possibility of that happening exist?
- What opportunities are there for my student to become familiar with the entire play?
- Drama is not usually a solo activity: how can I enable my student to work with other students in a drama context?
- What physical facilities do I need to provide for a) rehearsal and b) performance in an examination?
- Can my student 'inhabit' the role he/she has chosen?
- Does my student have the vocal, emotional, intellectual and physical skills to tell this character's story through performance?
- What skills, knowledge and understanding listed in the learning outcomes and syllabus for this grade will become particularly relevant in performing this piece?
- How does this piece relate to the student's own culture?
- Is it possible for my student to enter imaginatively into the 'world of the play'?
- How can I as a teacher ensure that my student understands that drama is about the entire person: body, mind and spirit?
- Do I really have an understanding of the possibilities for performance in this piece?
- Acting is not just speaking with a few movements and gestures tagged on; do I understand what it involves for this piece?

These are questions that you, the teacher, need to consider carefully because you will almost certainly need to help your students with a wide range of issues: the use of space, imagination, context, text, character development and the use of improvisation and other techniques.

Drama is a distinct and difficult art form and that is why in **Speech and Drama** we make it optional until **Advanced level** (Grade 6). For those who are comfortable with and enthusiastic about acting, the syllabus provides a number of alternative strands.

In order to help you make choices in Drama and Acting the specific requirements of the **Individual Acting Skills** syllabus are set out below. You can see at a glance what is required in this strand and you can apply the same criteria to **Speech and Drama**. So, for instance, if you are looking for a suitable acting piece for a Speech and Drama candidate, you might start by looking at what is required for the same grade in Individual Acting Skills.

Monologue or 'extract'

Before we look in detail at the specific requirements of the syllabus I want to say a word about the use of two terms that have caused some confusion in the past. You will see that, in Individual Acting Skills at Grade 1 the syllabus asks for 'a monologue, written or adapted for the stage', whereas in Speech and Drama at Grade 1 the syllabus specifies 'a prose passage or short extract from a play'. The use of the word 'monologue' is partially in recognition of the fact that almost every student actor will, at some time or other, encounter and want to use a book of 'monologues', usually intended for use in auditions or examinations. It has been part of the somewhat perverse snobbery of our profession that teachers have been inclined to look askance at such books while actually finding them to be very useful tools! Actors suddenly called for audition or students wanting to enter drama school have often been indebted to books of 'monologues' too. The objection to such collections is that they prevent the student from reading the whole play but this is to misunderstand both the intention of the collections (and we must include Anthology Online in these) and the nature of the modern monologue in the theatre.

A monologue is, literally, a single voice delivering a speech. There are several kinds:

- **A speech from a play made by a single character to another character or group of characters.** In this case, of course, one of the issues is the presence of the 'on-stage audience' and how this can be conveyed in performance.

- **A speech from a play directly addressed to the audience, whose existence is acknowledged in performance.** With such speeches, the examiner is, of course, part of that audience.

- **A speech from a play in which a character talks to himself or herself, overheard by the audience: in other words, a soliloquy.** Actors have to convey the sense of an inner dialogue in this situation.

- **A speech or series of speeches by a single character that constitute(s) an entire play.** A single speech will still be thought of as a monologue but a series of speeches or a very long single speech will be called a 'one man' or 'one woman' show or a **'monodrama'**.

Notice that, in all cases, the syllabus says 'written or adapted for the stage'. This is a further acknowledgement of current theatre practice in which letters, novels, newspaper articles and other such primary sources are made into plays and relatively short – but complete – monologues are written for stage performance. Trinity Guildhall is keen that its candidates for examinations in Acting and Speaking explore such material. Teachers and candidates may, in fact, wish to make their own adaptations – but if you decide to do this you should study carefully the learning outcomes for the appropriate grade to establish the expected quality of material and the skills that candidates are asked to demonstrate using it.

*You will find examples of all the forms of the monologue in Anthology Online. For more extensive discussion of the whole range of monologues see **Key Concepts in Drama and Performance**[3].*

[3] see Sources and resources

In the Speech and Drama syllabus the words 'extract from a play' are used. This is a somewhat more restricted requirement because it does demand that any speech chosen **comes from a longer play** and that the candidate is **familiar with it**. The play may be an adaptation of a novel, short story or employ other literary forms like letters and diaries and, at Grades 7 and 8 may involve another actor. As the syllabus does not always specify a monologue it is sometimes possible to join some speeches together, even though, in the original play, they are punctuated by a comment from another character. In the Anthology we have included an extract from Shakespeare's *The Tempest* consisting of two soliloquies that can be used separately or together for Acting in Pairs.

*The extracts contained in Anthology Online are examples of the length and complexity suitable for the various levels but you should consult the syllabus very carefully to establish the appropriate timings for the grade on which you are working. **Much of the material discussed below will also be useful for teachers preparing students for the syllabus strand Acting in Pairs.***

Drama choices required for Individual Acting Skills (with commentary)

Drama at Foundation level

Grades 1–3

- A monologue written or adapted for the stage

This requirement gives you the widest possible choice and is an invitation to range freely over the field of world drama. If you are based in the United Kingdom, it is likely that your perception of what constitutes English-speaking theatre is shaped by a sense of the history of playwriting in Britain and the influences from Europe, Scandinavia and America that have permeated it. You probably have an awareness of the various 'golden ages' of plays in English and a particular

reverence for Shakespeare. Immigrants to Britain have also brought theatrical traditions; there are, for example, very active Black and Asian, Middle Eastern and Chinese playwrights and theatre companies working in their own languages and in English, drawing on the cultural issues of their communities.

In some parts of the world the concept of English-speaking theatre was first introduced through colonialism and the existence of garrison theatres. This sometimes resulted in a distortion and neglect of indigenous culture that has, fortunately, begun to be addressed. Not only are there now fine contemporary playwrights in all the countries where Trinity Guildhall is active but also there has been a resurgence of interest in the performance modes and rituals of the societies that flourished in countries before colonisation. You will certainly find that your own country has such a performance history.

You will see that in Anthology Online we have included examples of plays and performance pieces from a number of sources outside the sphere of Euro-centric, English-speaking theatre and it is precisely this theatre that has been enriched by exposure to such previously unexplored modes.

Cross-culturalism is not just a recent 'fad' that people have embraced in a search for political correctness: it has existed for centuries. Just look at the effect of a visit to Cathay in *The Travels of Marco Polo* (see the Intermediate Prose section of the Anthology). We know that the first great textbook on acting and performance came from the Indian sub-continent, that the Turkish shadow puppets had their origins in Indonesia, that the Japanese Noh plays influenced the Irish dramatists of the early 20th century, that almost every major play in the English Elizabethan theatre mentions Islamic culture, and that an understanding of the concept of a 'sacred space' in Native American ritual or in the rituals of Patagonia is one of the major factors in the development of the 'found space' of modern Performance Studies.

The other comparatively recent development for which we should be profoundly grateful has been the explosion of good playwriting for young people. It is only 16 years since the international publishers, Macmillan, were able to add a volume on **Theatre for the Young** to their **Modern Dramatists** series, citing such writers as David Wood, Ken Campbell, Roy Kift, Alan Ayckbourn and David Holman who have created high quality scripts for young people[4]. Even more recently, the Royal National Theatre in London has organised a project known as 'Connections' through its Education department. This has entailed the commissioning of leading contemporary playwrights to write plays for schools and the subsequent publishing of the material by a leading publisher. For further information see www.ntconnections.org.uk. Writing for children and young people has also become the focus of a number of university courses and there is now a substantial body of work emanating from such courses and from festivals of youth drama. This all makes it vital that you scan publishers' lists and use the internet to seek out new and stimulating material. You will see that, in addition to the work of living writers, we have included some more traditional material. There are countless stage versions of children's 'classics' and these are still well worth consideration.

There has never been a time when more diverse activity in creating works of theatre has been directly available to teachers and students. Anthology Online provides some examples but cannot possibly begin to explore the new writing of your country in any depth. **That is the opportunity provided by the free choice at Foundation level in the syllabus.**

Drama at Intermediate level

Grade 4

- An extract from a play written in or after 1956 (This is also a requirement at Grade 6 in Speech and Drama)

Why 1956? Why do we define that date as a watershed? This is one example of where an event in the London theatre is used to define a period. Although we have done everything possible to encourage you to explore the drama of your own country, Trinity Guildhall is currently committed to examining work in English and it is inevitable that aspects of the English-speaking theatre are shaped by events in London.

1956 was the date of the first performances of John Osborne's play *Look Back in Anger* at the Royal Court Theatre. This event is widely acknowledged to have changed the course of theatre writing after a period of sterility. The play entered upon the consciousness of a post-war generation with tremendous force, 'sweeping' as one critic put it, 'the parlour maid from the London stage in a single moment'. It is significant that the scholar, John Russell Taylor, should have entitled his book surveying the new writers of the 20th century *Anger and After*[5] and the legacy of that revolution included the impact of the Berliner Ensemble's productions of plays by Brecht and the experiments in what came to be known as the Theatre of the Absurd.

However, students of modern Arabic Drama also date their revolution in writing from the appearance of the play *The People Downstairs*[6] by the prominent Egyptian playwright Nu'man 'Ashur, and many of the English translations of his and other Arabic writers make fine material for presentation.

1956 was the year of the Hungarian Revolution, the Suez Crisis and the first Rock 'n' Roll film, and for the young people growing up there was clear feeling that a generation that had muddled its way through two world wars was about to catapult them into another and that the only way to respond was to challenge authority through a new brand of artistic anarchy. For the current generation of students the issues may be different but the power of some of the plays written in response to that earlier world remains potent.

The fact that the syllabus selects a defining moment in British theatre for its 'cut off' date **in no way** implies that you must choose a piece of British drama. Indeed, this provides a perfect opportunity for you to decide what

[4] see An A-Z of teachers' terms and tools and Sources and resources
[5 & 6] see Sources and resources

are the defining moments in the development of drama in your own country. The intention is simply to ensure that candidates engage with the drama of the last 50 years or so and become aware of the many issues in the modern world with which drama is capable of dealing.

Grade 5

- A soliloquy or monologue
- A contrasting speech from a play

This is the first grade at which two pieces of text-based acting are required. Anthology Online contains examples of soliloquies and monologues and, in the section dealing with drama from different periods, explains that the soliloquy reached a high level of sophistication in the 16th and 17th centuries but had some origins in the Mediaeval theatre. The concept of a single actor sharing intimate thoughts with a visible audience in the theatres of Shakespeare's day was a revolution in itself, because those speeches often examined what it is to be human and provided a kind of microscope under which the human condition might be examined. However, at this grade you are not given any specific period of drama from which the speech is to be drawn and you might do better to range widely before making your choice.

The need to provide a **contrasting** speech may provoke the question: **contrasting in which way?**

This requirement is not intended to make your task difficult. There are many options, all of which are entirely acceptable; here are some of them:

- Contrast in mood
- Contrast in style, e.g. very informal as opposed to formal
- Contrast in period
- Contrast in language, e.g. verse/prose
- Contrast in character, e.g. age, occupation, hero, villain, introspective, extraverted
- Contrast in genre: comedy, tragedy, melodrama.

The intention here is to allow student actors to begin to explore and demonstrate their range of performance skills.

Drama at Advanced level

Grade 6

- A 16th- or 17th-century soliloquy (Grade 7 in Speech and Drama requires a 'play extract' from the same period)
- A 20th-century monologue (written or adapted for the stage)

Now that we have moved into the Advanced section of the syllabus the demands are much greater. Candidates are expected to have some familiarity with important periods in the development of English-speaking theatre and this may well take them outside their immediate experience.

The requirement to find something from the 16th or 17th century leads us to what was probably the most prolific period of playwriting in English ever known – and it centred on the London stage. The almost insatiable demand for new plays at the time of massive expansion of that city led to the building of new theatres, the founding of new companies of actors and the embracing of ideas from the Renaissance and Reformation.

The period offered to you covers the entire output of the remarkable innovator, Christopher Marlowe, and of the most influential dramatist of all time, William Shakespeare[7]. But there is a great deal more. The same period also embraces the careers of the most celebrated of French dramatists: Molière and one of the greatest Spanish dramatists, Calderon, both of whose work is included in Anthology Online and is now widely available in excellent translation. Teachers seeking a soliloquy might be interested, for example, in Calderon's *Life is a Dream* where Act 1 contains a remarkable soliloquy by Clotaldo that is, in fact, a long 'aside'.

It is worth noting that 'publishing' plays in this period was not a priority for the vast majority of playwrights. Ben Jonson was the first English-speaking playwright to have

[7] see Shakespeare the playmaker chapter

his 'works' published in book form during his lifetime: Marlowe only published poetry and Shakespeare had no part in the publication of his plays. Consequently, we rely on the work of editors and scholars to provide accessible versions of the plays of the period and this work is ongoing. Previously unknown plays are frequently coming to light and their potential for modern performance examined.

Dramatists of the extensive period we are considering are sometimes categorised by their dates in relation to the English monarchy: thus we may speak of 'Elizabethan Dramatists', 'Jacobean Dramatists' or 'Restoration Dramatists' or we may speak of the 'University Wits' or 'Jacobean Revenge Plays'. These labels are only useful if candidates know why they are using them and what characteristics they may embrace. That is why the syllabus simply specifies some dates.

Which dramatists fall within this period?

It may be helpful to you at this point to provide a list of playwrights whose work you might consider together with the titles of key plays:

Thomas Preston, *Cambyses*

John Lyly, *Campaspe, Endimion, Love's Metamorphosis*

Thomas Kyd, *The Spanish Tragedy*

Robert Greene, *Friar Bacon and Friar Bungay, James IV*

George Peele, *The Old Wive's Tale, Edward I* (often now attributed to Marlowe)

Christopher Marlowe, *Tamburlaine, The Massacre at Paris, The Jew of Malta, Edward II, Dr Faustus, Lust's Dominion*

William Shakespeare (see later chapter)

Ben Jonson, *Every Man in his Humour, Volpone, The Alchemist, Bartholomew Fair*

George Chapman, *May Day, Bussy D'Ambois, The Revenge of Bussy D'Ambois*

John Marston, *The Malcontent, What you Will, Histriomastix*

Thomas Dekker, *The Shoemaker's Holiday*

Thomas Heywood, *A Woman Killed with Kindness*

Thomas Middleton, *A Chaste Maid in Cheapside, Women Beware Women*, with William Rowley, *The Changeling*

Cyril Tourneur, *The Revenger's Tragedy, The Atheist's Tragedy*

There are four important points to note here:

- This list represents a very small proportion of the plays actually written by these playwrights, George Chapman alone is known to have written 21 plays.

- New scholarship debates the authorship of a substantial number of the plays from this period.

- Similar scholarship has revealed that many plays of the period were, in fact, the result of collaboration between two or even three writers, for example, Dekker is thought to have collaborated with Middleton on *The Roaring Girl* and Shakespeare may have had several collaborators.

- Most scholars agree that, around the year 1610 (Queen Elizabeth had died in 1603 and James I had come to the throne) there is a perceptible change in the style and content of plays. Writers whose work dates from around this time are those usually thought of as 'Jacobean' – some of them are mentioned below.

John Fletcher (collaborated mainly with Francis Beaumont), *The Maid's Tragedy, Philaster, A King and No King, The Knight of the Burning Pestle*

Philip Massinger, *A New Way to Pay Old Debts*

John Webster, *The White Devil, The Duchess of Malfi*

John Ford, *'Tis Pity She's a Whore*

James Shirley, *Hyde Park, The Cardinal*

Shirley's *The Cardinal* is sometimes seen as the last major play of Renaissance English drama and it is rumoured that the playwright collaborated with King Charles I

2. Making your choice

on the writing of *Interludes*. Shortly after, in 1642, The English theatres were closed and after the execution of the King by the regime of Cromwell, the English Court, including the young prince Charles, took refuge in France. Here they would have experienced at first hand some of the popular drama of continental Europe such as:

Molière, *Tartuffe, The Misanthrope, The Miser, The Imaginary Invalid, The Bourgeois Gentleman, School for Wives, School for Husbands, The Intellectual Ladies*

Note that these titles may vary according to the translation. For example, *The Imaginary Invalid* is sometimes called *The Hypochondriac* and begins with a wonderful soliloquy!

Lope de Rueda, *The Olives*

Miguel de Cervantes (usually known as Cervantes), *The Vigilant Centinel*

Lope de Vega, *Fuente Ovejuna*

Tirso de Molina, *The Rogue of Seville* (Act III opens with a soliloquy)

Juan Ruiz de Alarcon, *The Truth Suspected*

Pedro Calderon de la Barca (Calderon), *The Great Stage of the World, Life is a Dream*

With the 'Restoration' of the monarchy in England in 1660 a very different form of theatre evolved. Actresses were seen on the London stage and the plays were performed in theatres granted royal favour. A more elitist, society audience demanded plays dealing with domestic issues, of which marriage was by far the most popular. You will notice that Anthology Online includes an extract from Molière's *School for Wives* and the editors of *Four Restoration Marriage Plays*[8] list no fewer than 40 English plays written between 1660 and the very early years of the 18th century, where at least some major aspect of the plot revolves around marriage. The period also introduces us to the work of the first major female playwright in English: Aphra Behn.

Who were the other playwrights?

You might also consider the plays of:

Thomas Betterton
Colly Cibber
William Congreve
John Crowe
John Crowne
John Dover
John Dryden
Thomas Durfey
George Etherege
Thomas Jevon
John Leanard
Nathaniel Lee
William Mountfort
Thomas Otway
Mary Pix
Thomas Porter
Edward Ravenscroft
Thomas Shadwell
Thomas Southerne
John Vanburgh
William Wycherley

Every one of these playwrights wrote at least one major 'marriage' play and you should also note that several of them continued to write in the 18th century and may well provide suitable material for Grade 7.

Playing Restoration drama: a dilemma or a challenge?

It is perfectly true that much of the original quality of Restoration drama in performance was dependent on what, by modern standards, was an elaborate sense of display, a precise style of movement (largely dictated by costume) and an array of stage conventions appropriate to the design and function of playhouses. What we tend to call 'Comedy of Manners' tends to poke fun at social conduct and artifice, and an understanding of the social behaviour that prompted such plays is often seen as vital for the successful production of Restoration drama. However, as the great theatre scholar

[8] see Sources and resources

Patrice Pavis has demonstrated[9], plays in performance create meanings beyond history and politics and the process of giving new life to a Restoration play is not simply a matter of learning a few new movement techniques or acquiring a knowledge of the restrictions experienced by performers who *might* have been wearing certain types of dress in the original production.

Courses and books on 'period movement' are not difficult to find. Gestures can be learned, patterns of speech and dancing imitated and posture can be refined to resemble what we imagine to have been the way people moved and behaved. By gaining all this knowledge and understanding of original performance style we **may** produce a performance that has credibility and truth; but that knowledge must be extensive and accurate. The whole question of performing Restoration drama in examinations becomes problematic for two main reasons:

- Much of the subject matter is related to marriage and complex relationships. Such material may be entirely unsuitable for young acting candidates and better left until they are well into adulthood. Furthermore, the expectations of marriage lying beneath the surface of most of the 'marriage plays' are very different from the expectations of a modern marriage: modern young people are likely to have far more in common with the ideas of marriage underlying the plays of Ibsen or Chekhov than they have with those of Wycherley and Congreve.

- The gestures and movement styles so carefully acquired can still lack credibility if they are imposed externally rather than arising internally from the text. Unless a candidate has such a thorough understanding of the bases of physical behaviour in a play that it seems to be an integral part of the text, it is far better to revisit the play as, potentially, a new piece of theatre. There have been many fine and successful examples of recent

When I was wrestling with these ideas and, having watched a number of lamentable attempts to present Restoration scenes in a convincing way in the examination room, I consulted Frank Barrie – a distinguished Trinity Guildhall examiner who has enjoyed a successful career on the London stage and has wide experience of teaching acting students. (*Acting Shakespeare*[10] – the Trinity Guidhall handbook written by him – is an essential guide for students and teachers). Frank was adamant that, only if a candidate had the most complete and thorough knowledge of Restoration movement and style, should he/she attempt to provide an 'authentic' performance. Otherwise they should search the text and discover how the ideas and situations may be brought to life in modern production and *inform the examiner that this is their intention*. He said: 'I truly feel that the characters and speeches can certainly come alive without the gestures, movements and costumes to which we have become accustomed as part of the package.'

This final point underlines the necessity of envisaging any speech as *part of an entire production* and not something synthetically created for an examination.

productions of the plays of Molière or of Restoration drama that have translated the action into other periods, even into contemporary life.

The 20th century

The need to select a monologue from 20th century theatre almost certainly opens up the possibility of ranging very widely for your choice and, probably, into the drama from your own country. In this period we have the aftermath of the movements of 'realism' and 'naturalism' in the previous century and, indeed, the development of several more distinctive 'isms'. (You can consult the Trinity Guildhall handbook *Thinking About Plays*[11] if these developments are of interest.)

[9] see An A-Z of teachers' terms and tools, and Sources and resources
[10 & 11] see Sources and resources

Much of the greatest drama emanated originally from Scandinavia and Germany and was soon joined by magnificent plays from the United States. By the end of the 20th century, every English-speaking country had developed a body of dramatic work and, through international publishing, plays from around the world have become available to drama students and their teachers. A sense of what the period offers can be gained by looking now at some of the pieces selected for Anthology Online:

Vita and Harold by Anthea Preston

Anthea Preston would probably not describe herself as a 'playwright'; she is an actress who runs her own touring theatre company 'Images.' Indeed, she would be unlikely to claim to have 'written' this play but to have 'devised' it for her company to take to small-scale venues in arts centres, university campuses, arts festivals and similar theatre spaces. Vita and Harold is, in fact, typical of hundreds of similar devised pieces, often centring on the lives of well-known figures from history or literature and sometimes presented as 'monodramas' by a single performer or, as in this case, a small cast of two. Such plays are a response to the changing economics of theatre and are frequently based on primary sources such as letters, diaries, court cases, journals or interviews. They are often created for intimate spaces and are usually performed a couple of times in each venue before moving on. Vita and Harold was successfully performed at intervals between the years 1992 and 2005 by the same company. The play was never published and remains in the repertoire of Images Theatre.

There is, of course, nothing to stop you from devising similar material with your own students. Small-scale theatre companies, sometimes operating out of the actors' own homes, have become a regular part of modern theatre. The companies may have subject specialities or they may have particular issues with which they deal.

They may be committed to touring schools or colleges as TIE (Theatre In Education) companies and it is not always very easy to obtain the material they use. However, if you see work of this kind you will often find the creators more than willing to allow you to use their texts and such material inevitably makes stimulating work for acting students.

Madmen and Specialists by Wole Soyinka

Anthology Online includes work by Black and Asian writers and this is a rich source of fine drama. You may wish to seek out such plays and consider how some of the conventions of European theatre have been adapted and exploited by playwrights from non-European perspectives. Soyinka's plays address the legacy of colonialism powerfully but also enrich the fabric of the writing with distinctive Nigerian cultural features. Look also for plays written by members of ethnic minorities in your own country and at the work of theatre companies who exist to promote new writing of this kind. In the UK for example, the work of the British-born, Afro-Caribbean writer Winsome Pinnock is invariably stimulating and thought-provoking. Wole Soyinka has acquired the status of a 'World Dramatist' and his work is published and performed outside his native country: others, equally worth considering, may not yet have achieved this level of attention and you may have to go looking.

Promenade by Maria Irene Fornes

Whether you like to think of it as 'Alternative', 'Fringe' or 'Off off-Broadway' theatre, the message of this piece is that you should not confine your choices to the products of the mainstream commercial theatre or to the so-called classics of modern theatre. Highly experimental in form and in the use of language, many modern plays have eschewed the conventions of the commercial theatre by their length or brevity, their staging and subject matter. Some have been works of 'agit-prop'; others have defied oppressive regimes both in the political and theatrical sense and have earned the label 'underground' theatre.

The 20th century is the time of Jerzy Grotowski and Antonin Artaud, of Bertolt Brecht and Vsevolod Meyerhold, of Konstantin Stanislavski and Adolphe Appia, of Gordon Craig and Peter Brook and of Joan Littlewood, Alfred Jarry and Augusto Boal: all practitioners who rebelled against the 'deadly theatre' (as Brook called it) to shape new forms and intentions for drama that demanded new kinds of text.

The 20th century is a rich field for you to explore with your students. It may begin, for instance, with the Chamber Plays of Strindberg, written in 1907. In the last 40 years or so many publishers have taken the risk of publishing plays from the more unconventional sources of drama: much of it is, in the best sense, subversive as theatre should be if it is doing its job. At this level, you should be worried if your students are **not** viewing theatre as a means of protest or finding plays that deal with issues that concern them deeply or not selecting material that challenges the status quo.

Gilgamesh by Caravan of Dreams Theatre

Caravan of Dreams Theatre went under the name of Theatre of All Possibilities from 1967 to 1983 and that should be enough to inspire you. Making adaptations from Sumerian, Hittite and Akkadian ancient texts, this company was tapping into the very roots of theatre, narrative and dramatic literature and, at the same time, making something new and striking. Many modern practitioners have felt that theatre has lost its essential role as a teller of great and significant stories. The immediacy of an epic story and the multiple layers of meaning conveyed by such material make for direct and powerful statements in theatrical terms. In order to rediscover this potency, many writers and theatre companies have returned to ancient sources: Ancient Greece, China, the native culture of New Zealand, South Africa and America, legends and ancient dramas from Japan, epic poems from the Indian sub-continent and Anglo-Saxon epic poetry and stories from Sri Lanka, Canada or Australia are only some of the many sources that have been tapped to revitalise the theatre with a genuine sense of performance and communication. Much of this material is based on myths and explores universal themes; many of the stories have been told repeatedly in various forms but they bring us close to the process of making sense of our existence through drama.

You should note that, while the syllabus and Anthology Online encourage you to range widely in your choices, you will not necessarily gain extra credit for your students by selecting relatively obscure material. The most important factor is that the students achieve the learning outcomes appropriate to the level and feel comfortable enough with their choices to convey a sense of ownership.

Grade 7

- **A monologue written for the stage in the 18th or 19th century**
- **A speech in an accent other than the candidate's own**

This is the last specific period mentioned in the Acting syllabus, although the Speech and Drama syllabus at Grade 8 specifies the work of a 'contemporary writer'. Now well into the Advanced section of the syllabus, the period chosen represents an appropriately difficult challenge. The English-language and European drama of the 18th and 19th centuries reflects the fact of being written in the period of the greatest possible social change. The drama of the previous periods reflected a society that was relatively fixed in its hierarchy. The likelihood of any individual raising their own status through their own efforts was very small and, for the majority of the population of the countries that produced the drama we have been considering, life was perilous, predictable and short.

However, ideas that culminated in political revolution in America and France, together with the phenomenal changes to people's lives made possible through what we now know as the Industrial Revolution, all helped to create a world in which personal enterprise and choice became key factors. Although the 'goings on' at Court or in Aristocratic Society continued to be of amusement and interest to some, the theatre encompassed the emerging new world order and tackled some of the fundamental questions raised by the issues we would now recognise as 'modern'.

Changes in material life not only resulted in greater health, longevity, freedom and wealth accumulation but also involved more widespread education and literacy. There was something of a shift away from an 'oral' culture to a 'literary' culture and all these factors will be evident in the plays, novels and poems you read from this period.

The 18th century offers some of the greatest comedies ever written in English, starting with William Congreve's *The Way of the World* in 1700. Susanna Centlivre's *The Beau's Duel* (another play by a growing number of women playwrights) and George Farquhar's *The Beaux' Strategem* continue the tradition of marriage plays from the previous century. Your students may well enjoy working on Timberlake Wertenbaker's 20th-century play, *Our Country's Good*, which deals with a production of Farquhar's *The Recruiting Officer* organised by convicts and their guards sent to Australia. The plays of Sheridan – particularly *The Rivals*, *The School for Scandal* and *The Critic* bring a new level of sophistication to the period, as does Goldsmith's *She Stoops to Conquer*.

Later 18th-century drama included the rise of the ballad opera and the emergence of a more sentimental, domestic drama that reached its peak in both the melodramas and the 'realistic' plays of the 19th century.

If your students have difficulty in appreciating the enormous changes in the lives of ordinary people that took place in the 19th century, the following list of inventions might make the point:

1830: Lighting – a new improved form of candle eventually replaced by gas lighting

1846: Sanitation – stoneware glazed pipes caused a revolution in urban sewerage

1849: Dry cleaning

1849: The safety pin

1851: The sewing machine

1860 onwards: Processed foods, e.g. ketchup, jelly, custard

1863: The telephone

1870: The can opener

1870: Machine-made underclothes

1883: The typewriter – Mark Twain was the first professional writer to produce a typewritten manuscript

1884: Flush toilets

1895: Corn flakes (patented by Kellogg)

And, of course, throughout the 19th century the development of the railways and the steamship enabled ideas, theatre companies and fashions to spread throughout and between continents.

Either directly or indirectly you will find reference to all these inventions in the drama and fiction of the period and you will be aware of the lives of people living through a time of unprecedented change. The emergence of greater skill in medicine and the new science of psychology, the ideas of Darwin and the consequent challenge to established forms of religion all changed the perspective of playwrights and the newly-emerging middle-class audiences. These factors, combined with advances in theatre technology produced the kind of drama that the syllabus suggests as appropriate to Advanced level students.

A speech in an accent other than the candidate's own.

The ability to employ other accents is part of an actor's craft. Trinity Guildhall does not require candidates to demonstrate competence in Received Pronunciation (RP), but this section of the examination would provide an opportunity to use it if desired. Attitudes to accent have changed significantly in recent years and the BBC – once a bastion of RP – now celebrates diversity in its announcers and performers, both at home

Over the last few years I have visited groups of teachers at opposite ends of the world and there is one experience I want to share with you as an illustration of the significance of the need for contemporary awareness. On two occasions I combined a period of examinations with a number of meetings for teachers in very different continents and situations. As part of my visit, I inevitably found myself exploring the local theatres and, in both cases, discovered that they were presenting an ambitious programme of work by new, living writers. I attended some performances and was struck by the sheer energy and quality of the new writing. In conversation with the candidates and teachers over the period of my visit I discovered that not one of them was aware of what was going on in their local theatre at that time!

However wonderful the teaching offered, an evening spent watching the plays would have enriched the candidates far more and the teachers would have been far better off being exposed to new writing than listening to me.

We can all make the excuses of having no time or having no local source of new plays, but would you want to be treated by a doctor who was totally ignorant of recent medical developments?

Thousands of new plays are written and devised every year. About one in every six hundred is eventually published. It takes time and effort to remain aware but the rewards are tremendous.

and in its worldwide broadcasts. However, if candidates are going to achieve a sense of truth and authenticity in their work they ought to be able to respond to regional and national variations in accent.

Fortunately there are a good number of helpful recordings available for the study of accents, together with abundant examples on radio, TV, DVD and in films. Students need to develop habits of careful listening in order to pick up accents and need to remember

that accents are not simply a matter of pronunciation: indeed, by far the most important aspect of an accent is the **tune** and **pattern of inflection** of the voice.

Grade 8

- A programme of contrasting play extracts from various periods that demonstrate the imaginative employment of vocal and physical resources in performance

At this final stage before Diploma level candidates are offered the opportunity to explore and perform the works of dramatists from all periods and all cultures. Grade 8 Speech and Drama specifically requires 'a play extract from a contemporary writer'. Exactly what 'contemporary' means in this context has led to a great deal of debate in the past. So at Trinity Guildhall **we now define a 'contemporary writer' as someone who is living now or who has died within the last five years.**

Selecting prose

The requirement to select prose passages applies to both the **Speech and Drama** and **Performing Text** strands of the syllabus, and Anthology Online contains a variety of examples. Throughout the syllabus, prose is sometimes further specified as needing to be 'narrative', 'lyrical', 'humorous', 'for religious or ceremonial purposes', 'containing 50% dialogue', 'romantic, historical or science fiction', 'persuasive speech or public address' or, simply, 'contrasting'.

None of these descriptions or definitions should cause you any particular problems: there are examples of most of them in Anthology Online. The main issue is that **learning outcomes** must be conformed to in terms of length, complexity, sophistication and so on. Thus, the process of making your choices, must, once again, involve all those variables we have explored in verse and in drama. The Anthology encourages you to scan the whole spectrum of world literature and you should also keep in mind the vast range of forms in which prose is employed:

travel writing, letters, speeches, sacred texts, history, journals, diaries, short stories, novels, articles, biographies, autobiographies, essays, talks, newspapers, journals and memoirs. **All** of these, whether a branch of fiction or fact, are possibilities for your students and the greater the range of material they are exposed to, the better they will also cope with the sight reading tests. We do need to remind ourselves, however, that, whereas it could be argued that all drama and all poetry is written for performance, this is not so with prose – although there are of course exceptions which prove the rule. The novels of Dickens, for instance, were read aloud by the author at public performances with great success. Clues to performance may not be embedded in prose as they are in dramatic texts. You need to think very carefully about the qualities of the writing you select and their potential effect in performance.

As with drama, we need to keep abreast of what is being written and particularly the best new fiction and short stories. There is also a large amount of literature available on CD so students can hear complete books, stories or journals read by the authors themselves or by professional actors.

Enjoy the search!

3. Preparing for an examination

3. Preparing for an examination

A golden rule as you begin: Ask yourself and your student 'In what situation other than this examination might you offer this performance?'

If the answer is: 'We can't think of one' your preparation will almost certainly lack focus and may prove pointless.

At Trinity Guildhall we always encourage students to make use of their work in progress for examination purposes. So we would hope the answer to that question would be something like: 'sharing it with my class' or 'as part of a school concert or festival' or 'as part of a full production of a play'.

Preparation at Foundation level

Step 1
Remind yourself of the skills required
At Foundation level they are: *Audibility, Clarity, Free and Fluent Delivery, a Sense of Spontaneity, Creative Engagement with the Material, Awareness of Audience.*

Preparing a story or prose passage

Let's imagine that you have selected the fable of *The Tortoise and the Hare* for **Grade 1 Speech and Drama** or **Performing Text.**

Step 2
Find the essence of the piece
Recently, Michael Hinton made a published '100 minute' version of *The Bible*[1] and this involved finding the very **essence** of what that best-selling book contains. In a similar way, candidates must understand the essence of what they are engaged with before they go any further. In this case, what is a fable? What is it actually saying? What is it all about?

Step 3
Establish the narrative line
What actually **happens** in this piece? Students must be able to tell you before they attempt to learn the text. What are the **key words** that describe the seven simple specific incidents? What also 'happens' in general terms?

Step 4
Work on the characters
Who are the characters? What are their characteristics of speed and movement? Note the **key words** such as 'rushed', 'like the wind', 'quickly', 'plodding', 'steady', 'slowly'. Who tells the story? What does a hare look like?

Step 5
Define the action and activities more closely
The 'action' may be like the broad sweep of the narrative but the 'activities' will include tiny details of behaviour. Notice activities like 'laughing', 'nibbling', 'snoozing'. Make a complete list of all of these and ask your student to act them out if you like.

Step 6
Work on directness in performance
Get your student to tell the story and 'show' the action and voices at the same time. Find ways of conveying the physical aspects of the story and experiment with the best ways for them to share the story with an audience. Be bold and don't get bogged down in fixed rules about posture. On the other hand, ensure that your student is breathing easily without actually drawing too much attention to this aspect of technique.

Step 7
Find the overall pace and form
Ensure that your student adopts a very relaxed pace and then work on the many pauses and changes of pace that will bring the phrasing and narrative alive. Don't impose your own inflections but in order to vary voice patterns always take them back to the 'meaning'.

Step 8
Learn the text
Only when all this preliminary work has been done should you insist on the learning of the text. Then be totally demanding. Half- or

[1] see Sources and resources

insecure-learning is a waste of time for all concerned. If words are not known with complete confidence, the examination should be postponed.

Step 9
Review all the necessary skills
Ensure that the interpretation is conveyed through changes in pitch, pace, emphasis and volume and that the physical space is used creatively and appropriately. Ensure that your student knows who Aesop was, when he lived and what sort of things he wrote. This knowledge must be simple, complete and secure. No vagueness should escape your notice as a teacher.

Preparing a short play or play extract

This activity should be a natural progression from the previous work on a story: this is precisely why examples of plays and stories with the same themes are included in Anthology Online (**www.anthologyonline.org**) and many of the same principles apply to both.

Let's imagine that you have decided to work on an extract from *Panchatantra* by Kamala Ramchandani-Naharwah with a pair of students at Grade 2. There are also suitable sections for individuals and groups in this play.

We have given you a great deal of information in the boxed 'About the author' section opposite as an indication of what you may need to know **as a teacher** before embarking on the work of an unfamiliar writer. It is certainly **not** necessary or desirable for a candidate to have 'learned' this information but it will help you in enabling a student to place work in context. With access to the internet now widespread, doing research of this sort has never been easier, cheaper or quicker.

The inclusion of Kamala's work in Anthology Online is just one illustration of the international aspect of the work in which we are now all engaged. And that brings us to the first step:

About the author:

Kamala Ramchandani-Naharwar, playwright, novelist, short story writer and journalist, was born to an Indian father and Scottish mother and lives in Mumbai. A prolific playwright, her plays have been directed by some of India's most eminent directors, including Adi Marzban, Feisal Alkazi and Pearl Padamsee. Her two musicals on AIDS *The Big 'A'* and *S.O.S.* ran for over 25 and 50 shows respectively, and *Witness*, a play about the dowry issue has had over 200 performances with various directors and groups. Other plays include *Gitley*, a play about autism, *It's Showtime Folks: the Ramayana*, *The Magic of Christmas*, *Fairytale Magic* and *Yes Mother Dear*, which was the last English language play directed by Adi Marzban. Her play *Shanti* was shortlisted in the BBC Worldwide Play Competition in 1989 and her poem *Nameless*, was shortlisted in the BBC Worldwide Poetry Competition in 1990.

She has written and directed numerous radio serials for children such as *Zak*, *Enchanted Tales*, *Through the Garden Gate*, *Crazy Tales* and many others. These incorporate zany characters, wacky plots and plenty of music: yet, on a more serious note she also wrote and directed a 204-episode science serial entitled *Human Evolution* for All India Radio.

Panchatantra was first performed for the Festival of India in America in 1985.

Step 1
Establish the context of the piece of drama
What is the cultural context of this piece? Where does it come from and who wrote or adapted it? Is this the entire play or is it an extract? If the latter, where does this extract come from? Is it a scene from the start of the play? What is the essence of the piece? What kind of piece is this and what is its dominant style or mood?

Step 2
Who am I?

Once again we are dealing with characters who are animals. What role am I playing and how does my observation of this animal help my performance? What is my relationship to the other characters in the play and in this extract? What do I look like and how do I move and speak? Use any techniques like 'hot seating' to establish these details.

Step 3
Where am I?

What location does the stage space represent? Where are the other characters in relation to me? Where am I in the world and in local terms? What am I asking the audience to imagine? What does the text tell me about place and location?

Step 4
What is happening?

Explore any stage directions. What do they tell me about action and location? What is going on in this scene, precisely? What are the characters trying to achieve? What are their goals and their motivations? What drives them to behave the way they do? How are events impacting on the characters, including me?

Step 5
Show us!

Find ways to show the audience what is happening in the story. Make the narrative line clear by what you do. This is **not** about adding a few gestures or facial expressions – it is about telling a story physically and vocally. Use the stage space and make it your own for the narrative.

Step 6
What do I say and why do I say it?

Are there any words I don't understand? What am I thinking that makes me say what I do? What are the things my character wants to achieve through what I say?

Step 7
Learn the text and decide how to speak it

Make no attempt to learn the words until you have explored the entire piece over and over again, perhaps through improvisation, but **then** ensure that the words are so familiar it seems as though you have thought of them yourself at that moment!

Step 8
Review all the interpretative skills you are employing in accordance with the learning outcomes from this grade

For Grade 2 you will need to demonstrate mood, atmosphere, awareness of audience and apt use of the body and voice, together with clarity, sustained delivery and an imaginative response to the quality of the material. Are you achieving these things? If not, are you ready for this performance?

You will notice that the syllabus stresses a **thoughtful** approach to the work and this sense of consideration should be evident throughout the rehearsal process. Aim for the same level of absorption that a child might demonstrate in an imaginative or competitive game and remind yourself that you **must** be able to think of a situation outside the exam room where the piece could be performed to an audience or, even, to camera.

Preparing a poem

A note about poetry speaking

There has probably been more confusing nonsense spoken and written about the performance of poetry than about any other branch of our subject. The problem largely derives from the fact that most of us have ceased to experience poetry speaking as part of our everyday lives. Whereas we hear prose spoken and read every day, and we are constantly bombarded with performed drama through the media, we tend to reserve poetry for rare arts events, private reading or, more worryingly, for examinations. Because of this somewhat 'artificial' use of poetry we insist on creating absurd 'rules' for its performance; 'no gesture in lyric poetry' or 'no eye contact' or 'no physical movement'. It has to be admitted that these so-called 'rules' emanate from a Western, Anglo-Saxon tradition of 'elocution' that has little relevance for more than half the world's population who may well have very rich performance traditions of their own. Elocution had perfectly sound origins and we owe a great deal of our understanding of the workings of the voice to its pioneers. In the 19th and early 20th centuries, the 'recitals', 'recitations' and 'declamations' of poetry by famous actors were a form of popular entertainment. And these events were, most certainly, 'performances' in the true sense. But tastes in performance styles and methods change and the 'elocutionists' have left us a legacy of special 'poetry voices' and contrived 'rules'. Unfortunately, 'rules' represent an attempt to solidify what is, in fact, a fluid subject. Even as long ago as the early years of the 20th century the great W B Yeats was arguing for a more natural and dynamic form of verse speaking, as any attempt to establish a 'correct' way of presenting a poem in performance as opposed to an 'effective' way, runs counter to the spirit of poetry itself. There have, of course, been many attempts to find new ways of presenting poetry to the listener, many inspired by the poets themselves; poetry with jazz, 'beat' poetry, choral speaking, dadaist 'events' and rap are all examples. Poets like Dylan Thomas in Wales, W B Yeats in Ireland or the American T S Eliot are among those who developed distinctive methods of speaking their verse, but a new generation must find a new voice as mere imitation will not bring works to life.

While you are considering these points and their implication for your work let me give you three examples of where poetry is a natural activity and where, accordingly, some of the 'rules' by which we have been governed simply collapse and die.

As I write this I have heard news that the German cabaret poet, Hanns-Dieter Husch has died. Herr Husch was well known in his own country as a biting satirist and engaging performer of his,

sometimes very lyrical, poetry. Like Henry Normal, whose poems we have included in Anthology Online, his main audience was to be found in the cafés and night clubs of a major city and his performances invariably included him sitting at the keyboard of an electric organ, accompanying the speaking of his verse or standing at a microphone, smiling broadly.

In many Islamic countries, the poetry of the 12th-century poet Runi is still very popular. His best-known poem is probably the *Mevlud* which tells of the birth of the prophet. It is quite common for groups of women to meet in each other's homes for a reading and re-enactment of parts of the poem. This is an important social event in the lives of ordinary people and the 'performance' of the poem involves certain traditional movements and gestures appropriate to the birth and nursing of a baby.

Recently I went to hear a very distinguished contemporary poet reading and speaking his latest collection of verse. Some of the poetry would have been described as 'lyric' while other pieces would be deemed 'narrative'. The poet sometimes sat, sometimes stood, sometimes looked at us all and smiled, sometimes walked about and sometimes fixed his gaze on a particular individual. I only realised this *after* I came away from the performance because nothing drew attention to itself as a 'device'. The other point I observed was that his hands were rarely still and invariably helped to 'point' a word by tiny movements and gestures that seemed so spontaneous that, once again, I only realised what was happening because, for a short while, I lapsed into my 'examiner' mode and analysed what was happening!

Teachers who are interested in hearing poets reading their own verse (including some very historic recordings) will find the website www.poetryarchive.org very fascinating.

So now you have read these three examples, what has happened to those rules about gesture, movement and eye contact?

Poetry speaking is a different art form from drama or prose, largely because it is the **sound** and **arrangement** of the words that make the first impression. The 'work' being considered is invariably more compact and dense than drama or prose and is largely concerned with words, ideas and emotions rather than physical or psychological action. We may have to approach a poem in a different way.

With all these thoughts in mind let's imagine that you are preparing a student for a Grade 3 examination and that you have selected *School Bus Ballad* by the contemporary Australian poet Max Fatchen, from Anthology Online. Work through the following steps, using the notes in italic after each step as guidance.

Step 1
Read, listen and enjoy the sounds, images and rhythms of the poem

Remember that, even in a poem, there is still some story to 'tell'. At this early stage you may wish to let the student hear you read aloud. Ensure that the key words like 'clattered', 'bumpy' and 'swerved' are noticed. Be careful not to over-emphasise the rhythm.

Step 2
Now it's the student's turn to read it VERY slowly

Make sure that the punctuation is noted carefully. Watch the line endings, especially the 'enjambed' lines in several of the verses. If it is spoken too fast, try again!

Step 3
Think about all the images and underline and define the tricky words

There are many evocative images in this poem. Some evoke sound, like 'clattered past the paddocks' (enjoy that alliteration too), and 'backfired like a howitzer' (a heavy gun), 'the rain beat like a drum', and others evoke movement: 'gallop, tails aloft', 'swerved and rattled', 'outraced a bushfire'. Then there are

many quite sophisticated expressions that must be totally understood, e.g. 'importantly gave tongue', 'seats of learning' and 'obsolete'. Do not let a single word go unexplored!

Step 4
Think about what's really going on here

What is this poem about? Where is it set? Does it describe an event, or celebrate something, or both? This poem evokes an Australian landscape, but is that unique? What expressions mark it as having a particular cultural background? What scene of mother and children does this evoke? Do you have a school bus? If so, is it similar to this? In some towns mothers are now more normally seen driving their children to school in their big SUVs: is that what has happened to this school bus? What was the effect of the bus on the animals and people in the environment? Could you draw or paint a picture of the bus from the description in the poem? How do you picture 'Mum'?

Step 5
Explore the form of the poem

What is a 'ballad'? How does this very direct, narrative form communicate? Look at the rhymes and the lines and speak the piece as if you have a story to tell. The meaning and not the rhythm must dictate the emphasis. Once you let the rhythm take over you have lost the story. The lines of thought and not the lines of verse must be audible.

Step 6
Experiment with the best way to communicate this poem

Think of the physical position of the speaker: the sense of energy and narrative that must prevail. Encourage the student to try out different ways of speaking the poem, aiming for an engaging and fluent, spontaneous delivery. Be bold and try many approaches. Don't expect to 'get it right' first time.

Step 7
Learn the text thoroughly

Step 8
Review the skills that need to be employed and demonstrated at this level

Remember that this is the highest grade in the Foundation level and that those foundation skills must now be clearly established. You are particularly reminded that candidates will be asked to demonstrate how they have used pausing and emphasis if they are using the Speech and Drama syllabus.

Step 9
Speak the poem many times: sometimes MORE SLOWLY than you would imagine possible or desirable

You will be astonished at the nuances that emerge and the sense of mutual relaxation of the speaker and listener.

As with prose and drama preparation, the steps indicated here represent a minimum preparation needed to achieve an intelligent and satisfying performance. There are many levels left to explore. For example, in this poem, all the stanzas lead to the final four lines where a ghostly idea is introduced. So you may find yourself asking 'exactly when did the events described take place?' or 'Who was this extraordinary Mum?' You may wish to explore with your students the way in which legends evolve. As we have already noted, the apparently simple ballad form is used here with great effect but with quite complex vocabulary and subtlety. 'When winter veiled the ranges' or 'alarming shearers in the sheds' are likely to be somewhat outside the student's normal speech patterns or experience and will need careful explanation. The foundations of approach established at this level will be invaluable as the student progresses. Ballads are encountered again at a later point in Anthology Online and the modern use of a traditional form in this poem can help with more demanding examples.

Reminder

In all Foundation-level examinations candidates will have to engage in discussion and conversation about the prepared pieces. You should get into the habit of encouraging your students to talk about their pieces and the ways in which they have prepared them from the outset.

Moving on to Intermediate and Advanced levels

At Grade 4 and beyond, the Trinity Guildhall examinations require candidates to engage in a more in-depth analysis of their own practice in relation to the pieces they present. They are expected to be able to articulate the context of any piece they have chosen and be increasingly aware of the skills they employ and the form and content of the material being performed. There is no magical transition from Intermediate to Advanced level in terms of preparation, even though the pieces chosen will be increasingly demanding. Teachers may wish to provide their students with the checklists for preparation overleaf. The first section of this checklist provides questions to be answered for **all** pieces and this is followed by specific questions for prose, poetry and drama.

Checklist for preparation of examination pieces:

All pieces

- ❏ Do I understand precisely where this extract comes from, or is it an entire piece?

- ❏ Do I know when and by whom it was written?

- ❏ What is the historical and cultural context of this piece?

- ❏ Where does this piece fit into the writer's entire output and is it typical of this writer's work?

- ❏ What is the genre and form of this piece?

- ❏ Do I fully understand every word and expression used in this piece?

- ❏ Can I make a short summary of the content of the piece, demonstrating my full understanding of what is happening and the main points of this particular work?

- ❏ Have I ever seen/heard a 'performance' of this piece? Is a recording of such a performance available?

- ❏ In what context can I imagine this piece being performed if not for an examination?

- ❏ What factors will influence the way in which I decide to perform this piece?

- ❏ How will I use the physical space?

- ❏ How will I relate to my audience?

- ❏ How long will the piece take to perform?

- ❏ Who is the 'voice' speaking the words?

- ❏ How will my performance convey the essence and style of the piece without intruding between the writer and the listener?

- ❏ Have I really considered the difference between reading and listening? The listener has no chance to re-read a section, so what is the implication of that?

- ❏ How will I begin my performance?

- ❏ How will I end my performance?

- ❏ How will I ensure that my audience is totally comfortable hearing and watching me? e.g. how will I ensure that they can hear every word?

- ❏ Have I developed any irritating aspects of voice or physical performance that I should eradicate?

- ❏ How will I dress for this work and how will I relax before the performance?

- ❏ How can I ensure that I am entirely focused on my work?

- ❏ Have I ensured that several people have heard/seen my work before I offer it for an examination?

- ❏ Have I given myself time to experiment with and change my performance?

Checklist for preparation of examination pieces:

Specific points for prose

❑ Was this piece originally intended for speaking aloud?

❑ If my chosen piece is a speech that was performed in public, what was the intention and how was the speaker attempting to influence the listeners?

❑ How will I distinguish between narrative, description, reflection and dialogue in my performance?

❑ If there is dialogue in the piece, how will I handle the various voices?

❑ If this is an extract, can I say precisely where it comes from and do I know the rest of the work well enough to discuss it intelligently?

❑ Do I regularly listen to examples of prose being read and spoken on radio or recordings?

❑ If the piece comes from a novel or short story, have I thought about the specific art of storytelling and do I understand that, for prose, listeners do not have a rhyme or particular rhythmic scheme to assist them?

❑ What particular qualities in the writing attract me and can I explain them with examples?

❑ Does my performance respond to the qualities I have identified?

❑ Am I speaking slowly enough to enable my listeners to take in and process what they hear?

❑ If this is not a contemporary piece, do I totally understand the terminology and vocabulary used?

❑ Has this piece ever been dramatised for stage, film, radio or TV and, if so, can I discuss those adaptations?

❑ Have I read a review of this work?

❑ How can I ensure that the tension, humour, irony or other such qualities are exploited in my performance? Can I make the narrative gripping for the listener?

❑ Can I discuss the characters in the piece, if appropriate, and can I back up my opinions with evidence from the text?

❑ If the piece is written in an idiom appropriate to a certain regional or national accent, can I achieve that accent or do I want/need to? How does the text sound when the voice speaking it is from a very different regional or cultural background?

❑ What do I want from my audience? Do I want them to be entertained, moved, amused, persuaded, contemplative, stirred to action, riveted by a mystery, informed?

Checklist for preparation of examination pieces:

Specific points for poetry

❑ Was this poet part of a movement that has acquired a label, e.g. 'metaphysical', 'poet of the 30s'? How does that assist my understanding of this poem?

❑ Do I understand the metrical structure of this poem and can I describe it using the appropriate technical terms?

❑ Can I recognise examples of assonance or alliteration or any other such devices in this piece? How does this affect my speaking of the poem?

❑ Have I fully investigated the rhyme scheme? Can I describe it and respond to it in my speaking?

❑ Can I be sure that it is the lines of thought rather than the lines of the poem that dictate the way I perform the piece?

❑ How would I describe this poem if asked? Does its form have a specific name?

❑ Can I recognise, perform and discuss the images in this poem?

❑ Does the poem have a particular sound quality that I must utilise in my performance?

❑ Is my breath-control adequate to sustain meaning and form?

❑ Have I investigated the punctuation in minute detail and decided how that will affect my performance?

❑ Shall I stand, sit, move or use a combination of these in performance? Where will my visual focus be?

❑ Can I be sure that my speaking will be slow and varied enough to enable a listener to be able to envisage this poem on the page?

❑ Am I sure I haven't lapsed into a special 'poetry voice'?

❑ How does my performance reflect the type of poem it is? e.g. ballad, narrative poem, sonnet or reflective lyric

❑ Am I sure I haven't let the rhythm take over?

❑ Does my projection and articulation ensure total clarity and a comfortable experience for the audience?

❑ Have I experimented with the subtle shifts in meaning and effect created by different inflections?

❑ Do I know this piece so well that I have complete confidence in what I am doing?

❑ Have I considered writing and performing my own poetry?

Checklist for preparation of examination pieces:

Specific points for drama

- ❑ What is the point of this speech or scene?

- ❑ What is happening to the characters?

- ❑ At what point in the characters' 'journey' does this scene occur?

- ❑ How old is the person I am acting and what is the implication of this?

- ❑ What particular patterns of speech does my character have?

- ❑ Is the play written in verse, prose or ritual language, or does it attempt to sound like everyday speech? What is the implication of this?

- ❑ What is the precise environment of this scene or speech?

- ❑ What physical and vocal characteristics does my character have, and have I mastered these?

- ❑ On what sort of stage is this scene taking place? How will I use the examination space to represent this?

- ❑ When and by whom was this play first performed? How will my performance differ?

- ❑ Can I be sure that everything I do tells a story that the audience can follow?

- ❑ Will everything I do emanate from my understanding of what is happening to my character?

- ❑ Will my voice fill the space and my body respond to the needs of the scene?

- ❑ Who or what am I looking at?

- ❑ Who am I talking to?

- ❑ Will the audience hear, see and understand everything I do?

- ❑ Do I use these words so that they sound as if they are the expressions of what my character wants, needs and thinks?

- ❑ Have I got a total concept of what this drama is about and what I want to do with it?

- ❑ Can I give good reasons for all my artistic choices?

- ❑ Can the audience sense what my character is feeling and thinking?

- ❑ Do I listen to other characters and then respond?

Note: for all these specific sections there may well be points that have validity in other genres. Please notice that the technical language you may need to describe what you are doing is fully discussed in the two Trinity Guildhall handbooks: **Speech and Drama** *and* **Thinking About Plays**[2]. *A good candidate is not only able to prepare their work well but also able to discuss the preparation process and reflect upon their performances. In order to do this effectively it is necessary for candidates to be equipped with the necessary vocabulary.*

It is worth pointing out that many of the finest actors of the last decades – Judi Dench, Michael Caine, Cary Grant, Kathryn Hepburn, Spencer Tracy to name but a few – are often so restrained and economical in their performance that they do not appear to be 'acting' at all.

In contrast, young and inexperienced performers sometimes simply try to do too much. In striving for impressive effects their work can become histrionic and unconvincing. Students should watch as many skilled professional performers as they can – either live or on DVD, video or film – study them carefully and learn from them.

[2] see Sources and resources

4. Whatever happened to theory?

4. Whatever happened to theory?

When graded examinations in Speech and Drama were first introduced they were based on the examinations in music already designed and administered by the various examination boards. Musicians had decided that a typical grade examination would consist of some set pieces (possibly with some element of 'own choice'), some technical exercises, some sight reading and some theory. So our predecessors followed this pattern, partly to achieve a level of comparability and partly because they were convinced that our subject was as valid an artistic enterprise as music and worthy of the same treatment.

This model has served us pretty well for the last 75 years or so, but we can now see that it was flawed and inadequate in a number of ways. The most obvious problems are that the hybrid subject we know as 'Speech and Drama' has been joined by a significant number of other related subjects and that none of the areas of activity, including speech and drama, share precisely the same issues as music. You could argue, for example, that sight reading is an essential skill for a musician, but not particularly useful for all drama or speech practitioners. Whereas a musician may need to be able to sight read because a performance will involve reading from a score and may even consist of a group sight reading their parts, an actor may try many 'readings'. We can all think of situations in which it may be helpful if we can read something well at sight, in public for example, but there is really no comparison with the use of this skill in music.

The differences between music and our subjects are no more clearly seen than in the area we have come to know as 'theory' although we must remind ourselves that our colleagues in music are already shifting their position in this respect. Unfortunately, our subject, like all the performing arts, has suffered from the belief that a subject that is heavy with 'theory' is somehow more weighty and respectable than one that exclusively involves practical activity. Universities and performing arts colleges have led the way in arguing for the value of practice and the understanding of practical work as legitimate areas of enquiry and study. There has been a move away from 'theory' towards what is often termed 'contextual studies'.

Another major problem with the theoretical basis of 'Speech and Drama' is that it traditionally covered so large a range that it has now been taken over by various much more specialised branches of knowledge.

Theory provides us with a vocabulary with which to describe and analyse certain processes.

We want our students to think about what they are doing and the skills they are developing and it is the job of 'theory' to enable them to do this in an informed way.

When the most recent literature and syllabuses from Trinity Guildhall appeared, some colleagues were dismayed to notice that the definition of 'inflection' we offered simply stated 'any change of pitch in the voice'. This was hotly disputed by those who had come to think of inflection as a 'glide' of the voice within the overall pitch. The word 'glide' of course, implies that something is moving from somewhere to somewhere else and it is difficult not to come to the conclusion that a shift of pitch, albeit tiny, is involved. However, the main point of this anecdote is that we had taken our very simple definition from the work of Professor David Crystal, probably the foremost living scholar of linguistics in English. The rather beautiful concept of a 'glide' had been abandoned in favour of a more scientific and analytical definition drawn from the field of linguistics that was virtually unknown when our predecessors started trying to formulate a theory of 'Speech and Drama'.

An example from my own experience will demonstrate the importance of understanding the application of theory: Many years ago, when I entered my diploma examination in Speech and Drama, I selected the famous *Elegy written in a Country Churchyard* by Thomas Gray as one of my pieces for performance. At one point in the poem the writer speculates as to the lives of the people buried in this remote spot and wonders if some of them might have had the potential to be great and famous. After naming some notable people from history who might have had their equals in this rustic community, the poet continues:

Th' applause of list'ning senates to command,
The threats of pain and ruin to despise,
To scatter plenty o'er a smiling land,
And read their history in a nation's eyes,

Their lot forbade: nor circumscribed alone
Their growing virtues, but their crimes confined;
Forbade to wade through slaughter to a throne.
And shut the gates of mercy on mankind,

The poet then goes on to observe that the obscurity of the people in the graveyard might also have had its advantages. After I had performed this poem with the best possible voice production, speech and expression I could muster, my examiner began to question me about my performance. Mentioning the extract that I have just given you he asked 'Do you think you should link these two stanzas?' 'Well … not really', I replied hesitatingly (trying to cover up that I had never thought of it!). 'But you MUST,' he exclaimed and he went on to demonstrate how one stanza simply leads onto the next at this point in the poem. Perhaps we should observe here that the days when a diploma examination could become a 'masterclass' have passed. But it is an illustration of a failure to link knowledge with understanding. I knew what a 'linked stanza' was, just as I and thousands of other candidates knew and continue to know what 'enjambment' is: but I had totally failed to spot that this is not just a literary device, it is also a *performance* issue.

Once this term 'linked stanza' had become part of my *conceptual* understanding it became useful and meaningful for the future. For instance, my appreciation of the beguiling singing by Katie Melua of the song *The Closest Thing To Crazy* on a recent CD is greatly influenced by my recognition of her imaginative use of one particular linked stanza in Mike Batt's lyrics.

Something of a traditional area of knowledge has come to be associated with graded examinations in our subject and we can divide this into four main areas:

- Theory relating to voice production and speech
- Theories of language development and construction
- Theories relating to English literature and drama
- Theory of performance.

We shall discuss each of these areas in turn but at this point you should note that every one of them has now acquired a large body of specialist knowledge and practitioners.

There are, for example, those who are solely concerned with the voice in an area of rapidly expanding research.

When the opportunity to construct a new Trinity Guildhall syllabus arose there was a great deal of debate concerning what particular areas of knowledge and understanding were appropriate and desirable at specific grades. The first determination was that, whatever knowledge was required, it must be able to be 'demonstrated' rather than simply 'described'. Far too much so-called 'theory' has consisted of young people repeating rote-learned definitions without any concept of how these impacted upon what they were performing. Any definition must go alongside an ability to recognise its application.

Theory does not belong in watertight compartments and when we at Trinity Guildhall came to determine the nature of theoretical understanding required at various levels, we realised that **performance** issues rather than technical definitions and vocal mechanics must take precedence. For this reason it was decided that the first 'theoretical' questions would be concerned with pausing and emphasis rather than with breathing or vowels. Considerable research, thinking and discussion preceded this decision but it was felt that children who, with a little encouragement could certainly speak audibly, were much more likely to benefit from realising at an early stage that meaning and communication can only be achieved if there are pauses and emphases in the words being spoken. At Foundation level nobody is going to demand that candidates use advanced technical terms to describe the pauses or emphases they are using but the idea of progressive mastery ought to mean that by Advanced level they are using the terminology as a matter of course. The same would apply to the technical terms we use to describe verse. By a fairly early stage a candidate ought to be able to name the **type** of piece they are speaking but, by Advanced level a candidate should be describing what is happening technically in any piece they are performing. The real debate about theory centres upon just how useful it is for young people to know certain things at certain stages. There is little evidence, for example, that the ability to recognise a vowel sound at an early age contributes in any way to the effectiveness of a performance.

Let us now return to the four categories of theory we identified earlier and consider them individually.

Voice production and speech

This area of theory deals with the anatomy, physiology and mechanics of breathing and the production of sound. It often includes techniques of relaxation and vocal warm-up, and the achieving of resonance, projection, articulation and a pleasant tone. The focus is on the voice as an instrument and may involve a concern with speech faults.

Many of these areas are now the subject of considerable specialism and teachers need to keep up to date on theories of voice, many of which go well beyond the understanding that once formed the basis of Speech and Drama. The concept of 'vocalisation' is now embraced by many theatre and performing traditions.

The major problems with this entire area are that excessive concentration on the 'sound' of the voice may cause us to overlook the interplay between sound and meaning and that sketchy understanding of anatomy or physiology may do more harm than good, partly because the operation of the larynx cannot be controlled by conscious activity.

However, if our candidates are to achieve the audibility, clarity and performance goals necessary in a public space, they will need to acquire the skills of voice production.

Language development and construction

This area is largely concerned with the basic ingredients of language and its physical formation. In English the emphasis is on vowel and consonant sounds: their categories and physical formation together with an emphasis on how these impact upon the resonance, tone and articulation studied in the previous area of theory. To a greater extent, this set of ideas contributes to work on so-called 'speech faults' and may well also involve detailed knowledge of phonetics. We have extensively explored many of the issues involved here in the Trinity Guildhall handbook *Effective Communication*[1]. As a field of study the aspects that have been part of the basis of Speech and Drama work have now been much enhanced by studies in linguistics and language development. The negative effect of a focus on language and its formation in our work has been the misguided belief that 'Received Pronunciation'

[1] see Sources and resources

(RP) is the 'correct' way to speak and the basing of much of the classification on it. With Trinity Guildhall embracing a large, international body of students, this is no longer appropriate and regional accents are increasingly celebrated rather than stifled. There is still considerable value in understanding the mechanics of language in order to enable students to 'feel' the organic nature of what they are saying and to give it greater clarity and dynamism. We may no longer require candidates to memorise many categories of vowels and consonants but the skills in the effective formation of these sounds are by no means redundant.

English Literature and Drama

This is so vast a field that many scholars devote their entire lives to a small part of it. For us, it has involved the recognition of genre, verse-forms, metrical structures, rhyme and rhythm schemes, figures of speech, technical aspects of the use of language such as assonance or alliteration and the history of literature and drama in English. We attempt to equip our students to recognise what is happening in a piece of text and provide them with a vocabulary to discuss it. The major problem lies in knowing the appropriate moment to introduce a term or concept and, more importantly, how we do it. For example, if we have selected the poem *The Lion and the Unicorn* by Bill Scott for a student at Grade 2, do we point out the 'enjambment' in lines 4-5 or the 'alliteration' in line 6? It is certainly far more important that students understand and absorb what is going on in the poem before we clutter them with a technical term; conversely, it is far better to introduce a technical term when it arises rather than prescribing that 'at Grade 2 all candidates will know the meaning of enjambment'. Literary theory is a specialised area of study that has been greatly influenced by the set of ideas known as 'postmodernism' and you may wish to explore some of the ideas coming from this direction. We deal with some aspects of this theory in the Trinity Guildhall handbook *Thinking about Plays*[2] and you will find this provides a relatively easy way in to what is a somewhat daunting field.

Performance

If you look at the nature of the theoretical questions that may be asked in graded exams in Speech and Drama or Individual Acting Skills you will see that issues of interpretation and meaning are introduced well before questions on the physical aspects of performance. For example, a Foundation level candidate at Grade 3 is expected to have an understanding of 'pausing and emphasis', an Intermediate level candidate at Grade 5 is required to be able to discuss 'inflection', but an Advanced level candidate at Grade 6 is asked to discuss 'relaxation and breathing'. This does not mean that a Foundation level student cannot prepare for performance through relaxation or breathe adequately, but after much thought and research it was decided that the excessive focus on the physical rather than the interpretative was counter-productive and that it required the relative sophistication of the Advanced level candidate to be able to analyse and describe the mechanics of such activities as breathing for performance.

As we have noted in the opening chapter, 'Performance Studies' has become a major discipline in its own right and it concerns itself with how meanings are created in performance. We ignore this developing field at our peril. There has been a growing understanding that performance and the rehearsal process are, in themselves, a form of research and that the central task of the performer, whether it be a professional actor or a young person in a graded examination, is to create and help the audience create significant meanings. This may well involve experiments with inflections, pitch, pace, pause or emphasis or with gesture, movement, dance, vocalisation, text or improvisation. A young potential performer needs to know what options are available, how to describe them and, more vitally, how to employ them.

[2] see Sources and resources

I suggest now that you go back to the **learning outcomes** that we discussed in chapter 2 under 'Let's get down to making a choice' and identify the skills and theoretical understanding that are indicated. Don't forget that these will largely be demonstrated through performance and, only in the upper reaches of Foundation level and above, through discussion. There is no longer any requirement to write about such issues at grade level and it is one of the features of the progression to diploma level that a far more sophisticated level of expression and understanding of the theoretical bases of the subject are required at that stage.

Checklist of theory:

Foundation level

At this level a candidate will be able to:

❑ relax, move easily, breathe efficiently, speak audibly and clearly using resonance and articulation

❑ perform engagingly, employing variations in pitch, pace and volume

❑ *talk about*: mood, meaning, and the use of pausing and emphasis to achieve these.

Intermediate level

At this level a candidate will be able to:

❑ use effective vocal warm-ups and technique to achieve total audibility and clarity in a public space

❑ move with authority, ease and a sense of spontaneity

❑ use a wide range of dynamics to create meaning and moods

❑ demonstrate adequate techniques to be able to respond fully to the demands of the pieces

❑ *talk about*: character, moods and meanings and the use of phrasing, pace, inflection and intonation (these terms are sometimes used synonymously), and the context and form of pieces performed.

Advanced Level

At this level a candidate will be able to:

❑ demonstrate good breath-control, resonance, articulation, relaxation and projection together with subtle variations in the level and volume of the voice in order to sustain a complex performance in a public situation

❑ perform with a sense of ownership and mature understanding

❑ *talk about*: the form, structure, context and characteristics of the pieces, how effective voice and speech are achieved, movement and gesture, resonance and articulation, areas of literature and drama of their own choice, and all the factors that affect a performance.

It is assumed that candidates will use the technical terms used in the Trinity Guildhall handbook *Speech and Drama*[3].

[3] see Sources and resources

5. What's all this about improvisation and mime?

5. What's all this about improvisation and mime?

No decisions about changes or additions to a syllabus are ever made lightly by an awarding body. A great deal of thought, consultation and discussion always precedes the inclusion of any task or topic for examinations and there is a constant concern to make the work assessed relevant to the major developments in performance and education.

The inclusion of **Improvisation** may have taken some teachers and candidates outside what we might refer to as their 'comfort zone', but there are really no issues that cannot be dealt with if the concept is approached with an open mind. As an illustration of the continuing debate and enrichment in which Trinity Guildhall examiners engage I have included below the thoughts of two important figures: John Gardyne, the Chief Examiner, and Chris Young, an experienced moderator, director and educator. This statement was produced as a result of a series of Improvisation workshops and a conference of examiners – the authors begin with a definition:

Improvise *vb.*
1. to perform or make quickly from materials and sources available, without previous planning.
2. to perform (a poem, play, piece of music, etc.), composing as one goes along.
(*Collins English Dictionary*, 2006)

Improvisation is something we all do every day. We have to deal with unexpected situations and events with unknown outcomes and try to resolve what has occurred satisfactorily.

Most young children are expert improvisers. When playing, they intuitively create imaginary worlds and assign themselves roles, relationships and objectives within them. 'I'm the monster from Mars and you have to escape from me.' 'You're the cop, I'm the robber – catch me!'

In a broader theatrical context, improvisation is a valuable and recognised skill that has much historical resonance. It allows performers the opportunity to investigate spontaneous responses to unfolding situations and interpretations – often providing increased insight and understanding for performers and audiences alike. Good performing artists are able to integrate the spontaneous into their rehearsed work as soon as the unexpected happens. This is the moment when work which performers have learned or rehearsed in the past is recreated afresh in the present, when the actor can truly be said to 'own' the material performed.

One of the major principles that underpin the Trinity Guildhall syllabus is the emphasis on encouraging candidates of all ages to relate imaginatively and spontaneously to the work they prepare for examinations. For this reason, improvisation is an integral part of the examination requirements for grade and diploma exams in many of our syllabus strands, including Speech and Drama, Individual Acting Skills, World Dramatists, Acting in Pairs, Group Drama (Devised) and Musical Theatre.

In this context improvisation tasks offer candidates the opportunity to:

- demonstrate understanding of their chosen extracts and characters
- display an imaginative response to a suggestion or stimulus
- demonstrate additional performance skills while doing so.

Solo Speech and Drama / Individual Acting Skills / Musical Theatre

When setting the improvisation task in an examination, the examiner will select a subject that is well within the grasp of the candidates. There are no tricks or hidden agendas. The examiner is not looking for a bravura performance – just a simple, clear, imaginative and direct response to the starting point.

At Foundation level (Grades 1-3), candidates might for example be asked to act out part of a poem they have spoken (or song they have sung), to present a character from one of their pieces in a different situation (at home, on holiday, at school), to speak to a character from one of their pieces on the telephone, or to devise a short solo scene with a title or theme taken from one of the performed pieces ('the lost key', 'the enchanted forest').

At Intermediate level (Grades 4-5) and Advanced level (Grades 6-8), the tasks given will reflect the developing emotional maturity of candidates, and offer them the opportunity to display more sophisticated performance skills and to demonstrate a more complex imaginative awareness of the dramatic possibilities inherent in their chosen literature, songs or music.

Candidates might typically be asked to act out the role of a main or subordinate character in a narrative poem; to imagine and present possible scenarios that occur before, during or after the events in the performed piece; to give a completely different interpretation of a role they have already performed; to turn a large, public performance into a more intimate one ('Take that speech you have just acted and now imagine that you are saying the same words quietly to a friend while travelling on a bus') – or vice versa. In higher grades they might also be given a situation that picks up the dominant emotion of a performed piece (e.g. jealousy in *Othello*, ambition in *Macbeth*) and present a scene which explores that emotion in a different context.

The starting point for the improvisation will always be made clear and it will allow the candidate to be actively engaged in acting in the present moment rather than storytelling, reminiscence or description. In most cases, what the candidates do should involve some physical action although there may be effective exceptions presented.

In improvisations at any grade candidates need **not** feel that they have to bring the work to some kind of meaningful or ingenious conclusion. What is being assessed is their ability to engage with and present a character within an imagined world – and sustain that character until asked to stop. Candidates sometimes offer an 'ending' after 30 seconds or so which is in reality no more than an admission of the fact that they have run out of ideas. On other occasions of course, a pleasing and appropriate conclusion may emerge from the work and both examiner and candidate would recognise that as such.

Acting in Pairs

At Foundation and Intermediate levels candidates are asked to perform 'a scene developed through improvisation'. These should be scenes that have emerged through play, theatre games, character work or some other form of storytelling. They may be related to existing dramatic or literary works in some way – using the same characters as a starting point for development for example.

This work should be rehearsed and refined so that the scene has coherence, variations of pace and tone, shape, progression and reaches an appropriate conclusion. The performers do not necessarily need to have scripted the scene and learned their lines but they should share an understanding of how the scene develops and how their roles interrelate within it.

Spontaneous improvisation or improvisation with minimal preparation time applies only to Advanced level exams (Grades 6-8) and at this level we should expect some assurance and complexity to be evident in the work presented.

The stimuli for such work might be provided by a piece of text (a snatch of dialogue, the opening line of a scene, a line from a song or poem), by a physical object (a mobile phone with inappropriate text messages being discovered, stolen objects), by a newspaper headline, by a picture, by a piece of music, or by the examiner placing the candidates into a tableau which comes to life.

Examiners will be looking for evidence of mutual support by the performers and creativity in the creation of motivation, behaviour and language.

Group Drama (Devised)

The principles for creating 'A scene developed through improvisation' described above also apply to the Group Drama (Devised) syllabus, although in this case there will be three or more actors involved.

The requirement for spontaneous improvisation only applies to Grades 5-8 so again the examiner will expect to see some evidence of confidence and sophistication. The purpose of this improvisation is to test the security of candidates' understanding of situation, plot development, character and relationships in their devised performance.

Examiners might therefore ask the group to repeat the chosen scene but in a different location or period, or change the gender of all or some of the roles. Asking candidates to improvise around what happens before or after the performed scene could also be a valid task. Alternatively, the motivation of one or more of the characters might be changed and candidates would be required to adapt spontaneously to the change in the group dynamic.

And what do I need to know about mime?

Mime can, of course, be a form of improvisation: it certainly requires a good deal of spontaneous invention for its creation but the work can be rehearsed and polished to create a performance of considerable sophistication. Where many students become confused is that they fail to understand that mime is a type of physical performance in which spoken language is completely superfluous and should **never** be simulated. Advanced mime demands a very high level of specialist physical skill but the simple, prepared mimes mentioned at Grades 1 and 2 for Speech and Drama and

Individual Acting Skills and at Grade 3 for Individual Acting Skills need a straightforward, uncluttered approach.

Points to remember as you prepare a mime

- Prepare a clear outline of the 'story' being told in movement and gesture only
- Ensure great concentration so that the onlooker can trace the feelings and action in the facial expression
- Wear suitable clothes and soft shoes for work and movement
- Move from stillness to stillness
- Ensure great flexibility of the hands, wrists, ankles and feet
- Take every movement to its full extent
- Avoid clichés, like shading the eyes to suggest looking into the distance and avoid 'ballet' poses
- Use mimes of simple occupations initially: do not try to be too complex
- Sustain the energy throughout and create the impression of effort and force in movement
- Once you use a more complex theme or incident, build the interest from a simple opening and create the other objects in the acting space and in the imaginations of your audience by relating to them spatially.

When compiling the syllabus, Trinity Guildhall recognised that the art of mime very often involves a lifetime of study and so has confined mime tasks to the relatively early stages of the syllabus. A basic ability in mime is very helpful for the young performer but the main thrust of the work envisaged in the syllabus involves vocalisation of some form.

Assessment

All examiners judge what they see on published and accessible assessment criteria. While attainment descriptors for graded examinations are published in the syllabus, these are generic to all the tasks.

Specific attainment descriptors for assessing improvisation and mime are as follows:

For **Distinction** candidates should confidently demonstrate their ability to enter and inhabit a created, imagined world. The work presented should be credible and in role with a complete harmony of voice and body. Originality and inventiveness are evident and well-sustained. The performance is varied and displays consistent emotional engagement. Work will show a strong sense of progression with, where appropriate, an apt conclusion.

For **Merit** candidates should demonstrate a good attempt at entering and inhabiting a created world. Much of the work will be credible and in harmony with voice and body. There will be evidence of some clear inventiveness and variation, though possibly with some interruption to the flow of the work. There will be clear emotional engagement with the character, some sense of progression and a structure will be evident in the work.

For **Pass** candidates will show willingness to attempt and perform the task. There will be evidence that the attempted role is understood through satisfactory use of voice and body. There will be some inventiveness though its execution may be intermittent. There will be some emotional engagement though not always sustained and little sense of variety. An attempt has been made, where appropriate, to give a sense of progression to the work presented.

For **Below Pass** candidates will show a reluctance to perform. During performance there will be evidence of embarrassment with voice and body rarely in harmony. There will be little or no inventiveness and a lack of emotional engagement. There is little or no sense of progression and the attempt may be too brief to be adequately assessed.

You will find further help in creating your own improvisations in the following chapter, especially under the entry for **Workshop**. A number of source books for improvisation are included in the 'Sources and resources' section and it is vital that you keep your stimuli for this work constantly refreshed.

6. An A-Z of teachers' terms and tools

6. An A-Z of teachers' terms and tools

In this chapter we examine some of the key terms and modes of working that teachers preparing students for Trinity Guildhall examinations may wish to explore. Terms are arranged in alphabetical order for ease of reference.

ARTICULATION

Trinity Guildhall regards it as a basic, minimum requirement that, in work involving a spoken text, every single word is clearly audible and discernible. This accounts for 'clarity' being identified as a Foundation level skill.

There is nothing more irritating in public or private discourse than when words are not clear and a lack of clarity is, more often than not, caused by inadequate articulation. Articulation is the process by which consonant sounds are made and is achieved by the action of the 'organs of articulation' that interrupt the air flow to break up vowel sounds into words and phrases. There is extensive discussion of the physical aspects of articulation in the Trinity Guildhall handbook *Speech and Drama*[1].

Concentration on the mechanics of articulation can mask its purpose. It is articulation that gives that sense of energy to speech that can engage an audience. It is articulation that enables a text to be heard clearly, even in rooms and buildings with the most difficult acoustics. Articulation ensures

> Recently I was with a party of English tourists in Germany and one of our company told me that he had been amazed to meet a couple from his own part of London. 'Before I saw them,' he said, 'I recognised them by their lazy tongues!' As teachers of Speech and Drama we should all be enemies of 'lazy tongues': they are certainly not confined to parts of London!

that rhyme and rhythm are given their full value and that alliteration can be effective in a text: it is articulation that Hamlet is referring to when he insists that the actors speak the lines he has written for them 'trippingly on the tongue'.

Exercising the tongue, together principally with the lips, soft palate and jaws, should be an essential part of any vocal warm-up and, fortunately, there is an almost endless series of games and speech rhymes that can contribute to the flexibility necessary for neat and precise articulation. We probably all have experiences of what is sometimes referred to as 'through the teeth naturalism' in the theatre and on TV. The maddening indistinctness of speech in drama or public situations simply places an intolerable burden on the listener and devalues the nature of language. It can be avoided by accurate articulation. You may have witnessed speakers producing what they obviously thought were beautiful vowel sounds but still managing to be incomprehensible because their word-endings and initial consonants lacked the firmness and precision that give real dynamism to speech.

Faulty consonants are often associated with speech faults and there are plenty of sources for correction exercises, but imagine a candidate at Foundation level who has no particular 'faults' but who has elected to speak Charlotte Trevella's poem *A Drowning*. The second line: 'a ship's skeleton' already presents us with a classic problem: the reduplicated consonant. It takes a tiny but precise touch of the tongue tip on the hard palate, twice, each with its carefully controlled stream of air to achieve this succession of 's' sounds and the same challenge emerges twice in the following stanza: 'Parents stand on the cliff edge' and 'last night's storm.' If you look even more carefully at this remarkable poem by a young New Zealander, you will find that there are no less than 21

[1] see Sources and resources

uses of the consonant 's' and two more examples of reduplicated consonants: one of them involving 's' and the other the even more potentially difficult 'l' (the scourge of the lazy tongue!). We see then that a piece may, among other factors, be built around its consonants, all of which demand immaculate articulation. In the case of the poem considered here the alliteration used in stanzas one and two and the haunting repetition of 't' in the final stanza: 'Dawn light brightens / Tears fall' require a particularly well-articulated response in order to reflect the quality of the writing.

Key points to remember

- Try not to think of articulation in isolation from other aspects of vocalisation
- Work for precise rather than exaggerated articulation to avoid pedantic delivery
- Be prepared to find varying terminology in books on speech
- Include articulation in any warm-up exercise
- Identify possible pitfalls in any piece you are preparing and work on them carefully
- Insist that your candidates whisper their pieces before adding vocalisation
- Notice the energy used in such exclamations as 'yes!' or 'wow!'. This is the energy needed for articulation!

A great deal of time and effort has been spent by speech teachers in attempting to eradicate such 'faults' as 'glottal stop' or 'dropped h'. Non-native speakers of English may find this of little significance as they may encounter quite different problems in the formation of consonant sounds. However, all speakers need to realise that the quality of the writing must be preserved in the quality of the speaking and there must be a sense of clarity and energy together with consonant sounds that do not draw attention to themselves. When babies make their first recognisable word (that invariably sounds like 'dada') they are, in fact, establishing the basis of articulation and hence, the formation of words.

'Think of speech as a physical process whereby feelings, needs, and thoughts find their expression in muscular activity that produces articulated sound.'
(Robert Benedetti, *The Actor at Work*)

BREATHING

It seems almost absurd to add to the tens of thousands of words written and published about 'breath' as the foundation of work in Drama and Speech. However, teachers may well have become almost overwhelmed by the quantity of knowledge available to them and have concerns as to precisely what they are to *do* with it all! We refer to breath frequently in our everyday lives: if we have a potentially challenging situation ahead of us we 'take a deep breath' and when it is over we 'heave a sigh of relief'. Breath sustains us, energises us, calms our nerves, enables us to think, move and speak or enables us to enter into states of spiritual enlightenment and meditation. The association with the concept of the 'spirit' is common to almost all cultures and the acquisition of more sophisticated form of breath control lies at the root of most systems of training for performance, whether it be for music, dance, drama or public-speaking.

Textbooks on Speech and Drama or Acting invariably have their section on breathing and, as we suggest in the Trinity Guildhall handbook *Preparing for Your Diploma*[2], you should keep up to date on current thinking. The well-tried and familiar 'intercostal-diaphragmatic' method is admirably described in the Trinity Guildhall handbook *Speech and Drama*[2], but let us take the consideration of breathing a little further by going backwards.

Throughout this handbook I have stressed the organic nature of the performer's work. Body, intellect and imagination must harmonise in response to the demands created by the writers of the texts being used in order to make a joint communication with the audience. Voice and speech are no exception; they must not be thought of as separate from other elements of the performer's behaviour.

[2] see Sources and resources

Vocal centring is akin to physical centring and both indicate a deep centre for the imagination and emotions. Muscular tension inhibits voice and action. Emotional inhibition reveals itself both vocally and physically.

Put very simply, what happens when we speak is that an impulse is sent from the motor cortex of the brain which stimulates the body to allow air to enter and leave it. This air, as breath, plays on the vocal folds which are situated in the larynx, creating oscillations. These oscillations cause the breath to vibrate. The vibrations are amplified in the resonating cavities of the pharynx, mouth and nose and the resulting sounds are articulated by the palate, teeth, lips and tongue to create words. Additional resonance is available through all the hollow areas of the upper body including the skull and chest: these are reached by the conduction of sound through the skeleton and through the sound waves vibrating on one surface and setting up sympathetic vibrations on another. The resonators provide the **tone** of the sound while the **pitch** is determined by the rate of vibration of the vocal folds.

The focus of all our voice work should be on **release**. We should be freeing the breathing process, the passage of sound through the body, the resonating surfaces, the organs of articulation and the origins of emotion from the psycho-physical inhibitions which have been acquired as we have grown up.

Freeing the breath depends on an understanding of what is happening. Breathing begins with a signal to the diaphragm to contract. The diaphragm is a piece of muscular membrane that separates the chest from the abdomen. As a result of the initial signal, the diaphragm lowers and flattens out. The area around the lungs is then increased and, consequently, the density of the air in this area is decreased. The air in the lungs is now more dense than that round them and it expands, pushing the lungs out to equalise the pressure. By this time the pressure inside the body is less than that outside, so air enters the lungs via the trachea to restore the balance of pressure inside and outside the body. In order to allow

exhalation the diaphragm expands and moves up, increasing the density of the air around the lungs and the whole process is reversed.

We can see that the emphasis of the process is in the abdominal and lower chest areas. In order for the lungs to be filled to their maximum, the abdominal muscles and the muscles which control the lower, floating ribs (the intercostal muscles) have to be relaxed. The view from outside the body is of the stomach coming out and the lower chest coming up when we breathe **in** and the reverse when we breathe **out**. In spite of the certainty and clarity of this statement many people do exactly the opposite: their stomachs go in as they breathe in and out as they breathe out.

The effect of pulling the stomach in during inhalation is that people only use the upper part of their lungs, with the corollary that they attempt to expand the comparatively rigid upper chest by raising the shoulders. The result is a lack of breathing and voice control, together with thinness of tone and enormous upper body tension. There are three major causes of this faulty breathing pattern: simple tension that may be partly cosmetic (because protruding bellies may be culturally disapproved of) and partly psychological, chest and lung disorders such as asthma or bronchitis (and much aggravated by exhaust emissions), and intensive sports training, particularly for swimming, where the rapid uptake of oxygen into the bloodstream is paramount. All of these causes are likely to have interdependent problems of poor posture.

The first need is to encourage students to be aware of the **possibility** of breathing properly and for them to discover a **sense-memory** of the process. The second need is to release the muscular and postural inhibiting factors through relaxation. This is why all voice work, whether it be sound games for young children or a sophisticated advanced voice class, should be preceded by exercises that encourage relaxation. The supine position, in which the head is slightly raised on a cushion and the knees bent, is ideal for relaxing the abdominal muscles. Focus must be on breathing from the centre.

The above is a sketch of the beginnings of voice work based on principles gleaned not only from work in Speech and Drama but also from Yoga, Pilates and Tai Chi, all of which are now a regular part of professional actor training and voice consultancy. Teachers can develop their practice in a wide variety of ways provided that they understand simple physiological processes and their relationship to performance. But what is the point of all this?

Much improved breath capacity and control can:

- provide nervous energy, concentration and focus through oxygenation
- improve resonance and support projection
- provide greater flexibility in the voice
- avoid constant falling inflections
- enable performance of complex phrasing
- preserve the essential structure of verse or prose
- stimulate the entire body and ensure relaxed movement
- enable the performer to respond to any textual demands.

A working example

Consider the extract from *Alcestis* by Euripides in the Advanced level Drama collection in Anthology Online (**www.anthologyonline.org**). This is a very demanding piece and the demands it makes on the breath grow as it progresses. Students should aim to speak the first two lines in a single breath, even given the essential pauses after 'Admetus' and 'lie'. However, a couplet like this is a relatively modest requirement for a single breath. What are we to do with the following lines?

> Howbeit I now will ask thee to fulfil
> One great return-gift – not so great withal
> As I have given, for life is more than all;
> But just and due, as thine own heart will tell
> For thou has loved our little ones as well
> As I have ...

We notice at once the various enjambed lines where sense runs on to the next line and certainly the line of thought could be destroyed by clumsy breath. The most important issue here is to ensure that the voice has sufficient support to remain rising at the word 'tell' and, ideally, we might speak the entire section from 'gift' onwards in a single breath. If that is not possible, where would you mark the breath? Get into the habit of analysing speeches for their breathing places and experiment with what may become possible.

Key points to remember

- Concentrate on exhalation rather than inhalation
- Remember that fresh air and good ventilation are essential for good health and breathing work
- Don't begin formal breathing exercises too young. Make it all a game based on deflating balloons and other imaginative approaches to relaxation and exhalation
- Remember that great writers write with and for the breath. It will usually be obvious where to breathe if you study the phrasing and punctuation
- Breathe through the nose to warm and filter the air if possible
- Increased capacity is pointless without increased control.

'*Once we have understood its working we can gain perfect control over the breathing apparatus.*'
(Kathleen Rich, *The Art of Speech*)

CHARACTER

Drama, prose and poetry are frequently peopled by memorable characters and one of the major pleasures of engaging with such works is to enter into the lives of these characters. In prose and poetry, the performer must rely on description, dialogue and narrative: all of which usually involve an outside 'neutral' voice or, at least, a sense in which the performer only 'becomes' the character for brief moments. In drama, however, the situation is very different as an audience expects to be able to relate to, and observe the lives of, 'real' characters. The problem with presenting drama for examination is that a candidate may well have only a few minutes in which to establish and arouse their audience's interest in their 'character'. In earlier syllabuses what is now termed 'individual acting' was sometimes called 'character study' and examiners still take it for granted that candidates have closely studied the characters they are attempting to portray. It is also not unreasonable to assume that teachers preparing candidates for acting examinations have read and absorbed Stanislavski's seminal book *Building a Character*.

It is all too easy to talk about characterisation in general terms, so let us take a specific example from Anthology Online.

Imagine that your student has decided to present Trinculo's speech from *The Tempest* and is therefore going to 'build the character' of Trinculo. This part could be played by students of either gender.

Trinculo's speech marks his first appearance in the play and so the moment of entry establishes the character in the minds of the audience.

Always begin with three basic questions:

- Who are you?
- Where are you?
- What is happening to you?

Shakespeare provides us with very clear answers in the text:

- I am a jester at the court of Alonso, King of Naples.
- I am on an island where I have been shipwrecked and I have just arrived at that part of the island where Caliban, a slave, is hiding under his gaberdine thinking that I am some kind of evil spirit sent by his master, Prospero, to torment him.

- The entire court has been shipwrecked on an island en route from Italy to Tunisia. I believe that everyone else, including my friend, the butler Stephano, has been drowned. I survived by coming ashore on a barrel of wine. A storm is now brewing and I desperately need shelter.

So now we can ask some more searching questions:

- What do I say?
- Are there any particular characteristics in the way I talk?
- What do I do?
- Are there any particular characteristics in the way I act?

The answers demand that we look at this extract from the text very carefully:

- I seem to have quite a lot to say and I provide almost a running commentary on my actions, sharing my thoughts with the audience in a soliloquy and an element of 'inner dialogue'. The following words need explanation:

bear off – shield from

bombard – large leather container for drink

pailfuls – bucketfuls

not of the newest – rather old and smelly

poor-John – dried and salted hake (a kind of fish)

England – Shakespeare's audiences enjoyed jokes about their own country

painted – advertised by a painted sign at a fair

makes a man – makes the fortune of the owner. This reminds us that 'natives' were often taken back to Europe to be exhibited as curiosities or used as slaves or servants

doit – a very small coin

Indian – Native American. Remember that explorers erroneously thought they had landed in India when they reached America

let ... longer – express my opinion and no longer hide it

suffered – been injured or killed by

gaberdine – loose upper garment, like a large cloak

shroud – wrap myself up in

dregs – the last drops.

- So, I speak with the use of many images: some drawn from drink and others from the world of entertainment. I am clearly an 'imaginative' person and my speech is, in itself, a small 'performance'. I have considerable verbal facility; look, for example, at my use of alliteration in 'legged like a man' or 'there would this monster make a man'. My final words in this scene have become a memorable quotation and in later scenes I excel in quickfire patter and wit. I become very excitable when reunited with my friend Stephano. In later scenes I demonstrate an ability to make philosophical statements and witty comments on the situation and other people's behaviour.

What do I do?

- Shakespeare makes my actions very clear from the moment of my entrance in this scene. It is obvious when I first catch sight of Caliban, and my reactions to the prone creature are all indicted by my commentary on the event. I move, I sniff, I touch, I look and I let out my opinion. At the same time I react to the storm by cowering and eventually crawling under the gaberdine. In later scenes I take part in knockabout humour and, although I enjoy a drink, I never become so intoxicated as my two companions. I take part in a sub-plot that is an ironic counterpoint to the main plot.

Having considered the style and content of dialogue and the action in relation to Trinculo we find ourselves without some of the usual points of reference: we do not have any comments on this character from other characters and the only relationships we are able to witness are those within the comic trio situation. However, we do know that he has the precise role of jester, a particular sort of clown. If we need information about the nature of the jester in the world and theatre of Shakespeare and his contemporaries, we might wish to read Edward Marston's *The Vagabond Clown*, one of a series of fascinating 'Elizabethan Theatre Mysteries', by this fine author.

From all the evidence available to us, but particularly that contained within the scene chosen, we can create a vocal and physical performance that constitutes a believable 'Trinculo'.

In musical theatre and in dance, we use the term 'character' with a greater degree of specificity. A 'character song' in a musical, such as *I'm Just A Girl Who Can't Say No!* from *Oklahoma!* will establish the nature of a character rather than move the action onwards with an expression of emotion. Such songs often come quite early in a show in order to establish the nature and role of a character. A good example would be Nancy's song *As Long As He Needs Me* from *Oliver!* Through this song we understand Nancy's perception of her situation and relationships and this forms the basis of her subsequent action. In dance, especially ballet, the 'character dance' is an expression of a particular type, such as the 'sugar plum fairy' or the 'Arabian dance' from *The Nutcracker*. Here the focus is on the characteristic movement styles of the dancers rather than on the expressions of emotion encapsulated in the dances that concern mental states or relationships.

'Researching a character' has become a central part of drama training and the emphasis may vary according to the traditions determining their approach. The famous director and film-maker, Mike Leigh, insists on lengthy preparation through improvisation but this technique involves the creation of a text at almost the same time. Where a text already exists we need to search it for clues rather than impose some external ideas that seem appropriate to the role.

*'The actor does not need to "become" the character. The phrase, in fact, has no meaning. There **is** no character. There are only lines*

upon a page. They are lines of dialogue meant to be said by the actor. When he or she says them simply, in an attempt to achieve an object more or less like that suggested by the author, the audience sees an **illusion** of a character upon the stage.'

(David Mamet, *True and False*)

DEMONSTRATION

The syllabus uses this word several times but in slightly varying contexts.

In any examination on an aspect of performance, the onus is on candidates to 'demonstrate' their skills, knowledge and understanding through the pieces they present and 'demonstrate' their ability to discuss them. They may also be required to demonstrate a process or technique or their approach to a particular task.

In the field of Communication Studies the term 'demonstration speech' has a quite specific meaning. This is a speech in which the presenter clearly explains either a process (such as the preparation of a particular dish) or the qualities of a product (such as a new gadget). Such speeches are of vital importance to potential salespeople or to those who wish to impart skills that may range from hairdressing to the use of computers. A 'demonstration speech', requires all the preparation of material, consideration of audience, use of practical activity and total clarity that any student of Communication Skills should be able to organise. The apparently simple task of 'showing' someone how something is done is often, in fact, fraught with difficulties. Experienced dance teachers, for example, will know that if they attempt to teach a dance step or choreographic sequence facing their class, there are immediate problems of perception. Quite literally, the perception that we have depends on our 'point of view' and we recognise this by using the same image to express the idea in such expressions as 'from where I stand', 'I approach it from this angle' or 'from my perspective'.

Of course, all teachers and directors know how it feels to say 'Do it like this!' and then to demonstrate! The danger with this quick solution is that, unless it is a straightforward technique being demonstrated, students will simply imitate their teachers and produce a 'second hand' performance. However, there are times when explanation must be accompanied by demonstration in order to clarify a point.

'Most Asian performance techniques are passed to students by performers themselves, for in the traditional arts there is no such role as a director.'

(Paul Allain, *The Art of Stillness*)

The problems associated with teaching and explanation through demonstration are well illustrated through the following drama game/role play that never seems to fail to engage and provoke lively activity from the participants:

Divide your class or group into smaller groups of 4–6 members.

Give each group member a number.

Each group member will be required to teach a task through demonstration to the rest of the group, who will join in accordingly. Props, situations and even the skill in question may have to be imagined. The group members begin their demonstration when their number is called out. There is no need to prolong the activity: allow a few minutes for each task. Group members will not know their task until the teacher/tutor calls it out with their number:

e.g. 'Number one: you are teaching a relaxation exercise to your group.'

'Change! Number two: you are teaching your group how to be a fashion model.'

'Change! Number three: you are instructing your group in military drill.'

'Change! Number four: you are teaching meditation.'

'Change! Number five: you are teaching basic flower arranging.'

And so on. Vary the activity according to the age and cultural background of your class.

Checklist for use of term 'demonstration' in syllabus:

Speech and Drama: Grades 3-5

■ *'Candidates will be asked to demonstrate understanding of the prepared pieces and the use of ...'*

By demonstration here, the syllabus means an ability to give examples from the text and their performance together with an ability to talk about the context of the pieces, both in terms of their being extracts from longer works or their place in the work of that author. An understanding of some historical and social context may be relevant at Grades 4 and 5 (Intermediate level).

Speech and Drama: Grade 8

■ *'A prepared talk, with some demonstration ...'*

The term 'demonstration', here may include performing a brief extract, giving a few working examples, showing how a movement or gesture works in a piece or playing a recording (audio or visual) of an example. Visual aids may be appropriate and may include, but not be dominated by, PowerPoint.

World Dramatists: Grade 4

■ *'Tell the story of the play, or another, without notes, emphasising highlights and its potential for the stage, in an imaginative manner with some demonstration, to an imagined audience.'*

This task is available to individuals, pairs and groups: this, of course, will affect the nature of the demonstration possible. By far the best way of approaching this task is for candidates to imagine that their audience is a potential cast for the play for which they are preparing a production. They can then show set designs, staging ideas or costume sketches together with providing practical examples of key moments

in the action or demonstrating the performance style that they envisage. The basic aim is to enthuse the imaginary cast for the production ahead of them.

World Dramatists: Grade 7

■ *'A prepared talk with some demonstration on the playwright's employment of **one** of the following: characterisation and plot, ideas and themes, language, mood, style, staging or on the quality, interpretation and textual freedoms in filmed versions.'*

The important point here is for candidates to illustrate whatever points they wish to make with examples from the works in question. If the chosen topic is related directly to the text of the plays then the demonstration should consist of practical examples acted out, spoken or shown in a recording. Staging or filmic issues are best dealt with by visual images but on their own these may not be sufficient and any showing should normally be accompanied by commentary and explanation.

Shakespeare: Grade 7

■ *'A prepared talk, with some demonstration on Shakespeare's use of **one** of the following: the chorus, the dumb show, song, masque and dance, disguise.'*

As with World Dramatists this requires a fairly sophisticated use of demonstration. Examples from the text can be acted or spoken and 'dumb show' partly acted out; music, masque and dance can all be performed but also demonstrated through recorded media. Once again, the onus is on candidates to demonstrate their knowledge and understanding by providing practical examples that they can show and discuss.

EXPRESSION

We most often notice expression by its absence. We speak of 'expressionless' voices, 'vacant expressions' and, in some desperation, we ask students to 'put some expression' into their work. Expression, like gesture, is not something to be tagged on to an existing performance; it should arise organically in the performance process and should be directly related to the ideas, moods, meanings, images and forms in a text. The performer's instrument is an expressive entity that is capable of responding to the demands of language and feelings, imaginary situations and real issues that may be encountered in any piece they may be working with. Audible print is not a minimum requirement for a performance at any level, there must be intention to express the essence of the work and, indeed, to involve an element of self-expression. One of the seminal books on the teaching of Speech and Drama in the early years of the last century was E J Burton's *Teaching English Through Self-Expression* and it enshrined an essential aspect of our subject: that we come to an understanding of literature and drama through having something to say ourselves; we then become an effective medium through which a writer's ideas and thoughts can be conveyed.

We have constantly emphasised the holistic nature of the performer's body and voice in this handbook. But we do need to recognise that, in order to become a thoroughly expressive instrument our body must be trained to respond effectively to any demands placed upon it in performance. A basic requirement is a voice that is a pleasure to listen to and a body that moves with some elegance and ease. There must be a sense that body and voice are under careful control and yet are entirely flexible. We should recognise that all forms of actor-training (and there are many of them) aim to create an expressive and responsive performer.

Listening to the speaking of a text that lacks expression reminds us of the various elements we can use to imbue words with far greater varieties of meaning and interest. It is the first duty of a performer to 'engage' their audience, so what are the main means of expression for this task? For the moment I am going to assume that we are considering a text-based performance in the tradition of Western, English-speaking performance: teachers must be aware that there are many other valuable performance traditions, very often based on extensive physicality, that may be employed.

The main means of vocal expression:

- Emphasis
- Pause
- Pace
- Inflection
- Pitch
- Power and volume
- Tone
- Understatement
- Focus and projection.

Which leads us on to

Non-vocal expression:

- Eye contact
- Posture and stance
- Gesture and forms of movement, including dance or ritual movement
- Facial expression
- Tension and relaxation in the body.

Many of these issues have already been discussed or will be considered in other sections and they present the performer with a bewildering number of choices. Expression is an integral part of understanding and the making of meanings. Candidates must be aware of the potential in their voices and bodies in order to apply the means of expression effectively. In everyday life and for a variety of social reasons we employ a very narrow range of expressive potential in our meetings and conversations, so it may be necessary to notate a piece for 'expression' as we prepare it for performance. One of the major considerations is that extracts and pieces offered for examination involve complex ideas and emotions. These require time for an audience to absorb and process. Thus, the issues of pace and pause are paramount. At the same time, we can express so much simply by the way we stand or sit, and we convey volumes by our eyes and visual focus.

'Dramatic or theatrical expression, like any artistic expression, is conceived, according to the classical view, as an externalisation, as a fore-grounding of deep meaning and hidden elements, and thus as movement from inside out.'

(Patrice Pavis, *Dictionary of the Theatre: Terms, Concepts and Analysis*)

FLUENCY

The learning outcomes for Foundation level include the concept of 'free and fluent delivery' and all teachers would recognise the desirability of a sense of fluency in their candidate's work. Many important books on voice production have focused on the idea of 'freeing' the natural voice and, as we have seen in the entry on Breathing, this is a basic aim of the relaxation and warm-up that are recommended. The idea of fluency suggests a lack of restriction and inhibition: a need to rid ourselves of 'blocks' that get in the way of attempts to express ideas and emotions. These inhibitions may be physical or mental; they may stem from a reluctance to open the mouth widely enough or a sense of inadequacy or nerves that prevent us from functioning at our best. A lack of fluency (and, as with 'expression', we notice it most by its absence) may also be a result of inadequate mastery of the material. If our students fail to internalise the material they are presenting they are unlikely to give any sense of fluency in their delivery.

To sum up, then, **we can achieve fluency through:**

- **relaxation: particularly of the neck, torso, jaw and shoulders**
- **breath-control and capacity**
- **careful articulation**

- **flexibility of all the organs of articulation**
- **projection and conscious, organic moulding of vowel sounds without exaggeration**
- **total comprehension and mastery of material**
- **thorough learning of the text.**

*'But I must emphasise at this point that these [breathing and speech] exercises must be carried out **well away from any expressive speech work** … if you do them seriously you will not have time to think about their possible use in a poem you are preparing to speak. And when you come to the poem, the same rule must apply. You will think **only of the poem** and nothing at **all** about breath supply, consonant clarity or anything of that sort. Only of the poem'.*

(Betty Mulcahy, *How to Speak a Poem*)

GESTURE

Writing in Berlin in the 1930s, the great director and playwright Bertolt Brecht said 'Everything to do with emotions has to be externalised, that is to say, developed into a gesture'. 19th-century elocutionists classified gestures as belonging to the Colloquial radius, Rhetorical radius or Epic radius and studies in Ancient Indian and Japanese performance styles reveal constant attempts to develop and codify an expressive physical language. And yet we seem to be uneasy with the concept of gesture and become worried about its appropriateness, especially in the performance of poetry.

As the previous paragraph indicates, there are many traditions of gesture and attitudes to gesture in the modern world. From what we can tell by research into eye-witness accounts, some of the performances of poetry by great 19th-century actors in the English theatre were much closer to what we would now call 'acting' than the rather restrained and restricted methods of speaking poetry that have become common in our time. On the other hand, the desire for a much more natural mode of delivery and a concern to 'let the words speak for themselves' has shaped our approach so that some teachers and practitioners now wish to impose rules such as 'no gesture in lyric poetry'. Compare this dictum with Brecht's statement above!

The tradition of free expression and lyricism developed by the educational pioneer, Rudolph Steiner (who wrote a book entitled *Speech and Drama*), advocates that poetry is virtually danced in performance and in many centres where Chinese or Indian culture are the predominant influences, it is quite common for poetry speaking to be accompanied by carefully coded and stylised gesture arising from the situations and ideas contained in the poem.

What we clearly cannot do is to impose our own particular cultural attitude to gesture onto students who have their own traditions and values, even if they are working in the medium of English. We should remind ourselves that the English theatre has long presented drama from Ancient Greece in translation without any real concept or knowledge of the performance style of the original!

The most important single factor that we have been reminded of through such practice as the Butoh dance of Japan, is that gesture must arise from a process of distillation that involves stillness and isolation. Unless we recognise that stillness is not a negative state but a state of positive energy we cannot appreciate its potency. A great deal of verse-speaking, for example, seems to demand absolute stillness but that is not just an absence of movement: it is a gathering of focus and physical energy that communicates through its intensity. Effective communication through movement also pre-supposes that each limb or expressive part of the body can be isolated to function efficiently in its own right as well as in conjunction with others.

Non-verbal communication is a field of study in itself and, like every other aspect of performance, demands careful observation from students. Many of the gestures used

in examination performance are little more than clichés with no roots in the emotion or psychological state of the characters or content of the text. Some plays, for example, demand highly stylised movement whereas others demand naturalistic behaviour: superimposing one onto the other is a disaster. How often have we seen sincere young performers in a 'realistic' piece, looking into the distance with their hand shading their eyes, in a balletic pose?

*'The actor is attentive to both expressing his emotions and giving **shape** to emotions through gesture.'*

(Patrice Pavis, *Dictionary of the Theatre: Terms, Concepts and Analysis*)

HEROIC COUPLET

This is one of the literary terms that candidates are invited to discuss at Grade 8 in Speech and Drama. As you teach your students to recognise, understand and use the heroic couplet, you will inevitably find that you introduce them to other useful terms in the process.

The heroic couplet consists of a pair of rhyming pentameters and was first introduced in English poetry by Geoffrey Chaucer (c. 1340-1400). Take this couplet from the **Prologue of the Nonne Prestes Tale** in Chaucer's **The Canterbury Tales**:

'Ho!' quod the knight, 'good sir, no more of this,
'That ye han seyd is right y-nough, y-wis.'

This lively metre and rhyme scheme sustains this remarkable work throughout and is sometimes nicknamed 'the riding rhyme' accordingly. In this example you will notice the **caesura** in the medial (middle) position of the first line: a common feature of the heroic couplet.

In English poetry, the heroic couplet was extensively employed in the neo-classical poems of Crabbe, Dryden and Pope: achieving a certain elegance and formality and providing an especially suitable means of creating an epigrammatic and memorable statement. Here are some lines from Dryden's **A Poem on the Prince**:

Our Vows are heard betimes! And Heaven takes care
To grant, before we can conclude the Pray'r:
Preventing angels met it half the way,
And sent us back to Praise, who came to Pray.

We see again the **caesura** in the first line and that the first couplet is an **open couplet** with an **enjambed** line-end to the first **pentameter**. The second couplet is a **closed couplet** with each pentameter **end-stopped**.

Note how many terms your student now needs to know in order to discuss heroic couplets!

Alexander Pope (1688-1744) was the master of biting satire and the witheringly economic heroic couplet:

Thus unlamented pass the proud away,
The gaze of fools, and pageant of a day!
So perish all whose breast ne'er learn'd to glow
For others' good, or melt at others' woe!

(from **Elegy to the Memory of an Unfortunate Lady**)

- Ask your students to spot the **closed** and **open couplets**, the **enjambed line** and the end-stopped lines.

- Now compare these examples with Joan Goodall's poem *Love in Darkness* in Anthology Online and notice her use of the heroic couplet in a contemporary poem.

Dryden also used the heroic couplet extensively in his plays. In the prologue to **Amphitryon**, the leading actress (Mrs Bracegirdle in the first production) addresses the male audience exclusively in heroic couplets. She concludes:

Recant betimes, 'tis prudence to submit;
Our sex is still your overmatch in wit.
We never fail, with new, successful arts,
To make fine fools of you and all your parts!

- Compare this with the notes on marriage plays in Anthology Online.

- Now look at the translation of Agnes's speech from Molière's *School for Wives* in Anthology Online. Why do you think the translator has used heroic couplets here?

Dryden uses heroic couplets spasmodically for the dialogue in *Amphitryon* but it seems clumsy when compared with Shakespeare's handling in such plays as **A Midsummer Night's Dream**. Not only does the playwright use heroic couplets for some memorable solo speeches, he also uses them as dialogue between two characters. Look at these examples:

Here is Helena, one of the young lovers, bemoaning the fact that her friend Hermia seems to be much more successful with Demetrius:

HELENA: How happy some oe'r other some can be!
Through Athens I am thought as fair as she.
But what of that? Demetrius thinks not so;
He will not know what all but he do know.

And here are Helena and Hermia in dialogue about the problem with Demetrius:

HERMIA: I frown upon him, yet he loves me still.

HELENA: O that your frowns would teach my smiles such skill!

HERMIA: I give him curses, yet he gives me love.

HELENA: O that my prayers could such affection move!

HERMIA: The more I hate, the more he follows me.

HELENA: The more I love, the more he hateth me.

HERMIA: His folly, Helena, is no fault of mine.

HELENA: None but your beauty. Would that fault were mine!

- Note where Shakespeare alters the rhythmic structure and number of feet in one line to break the potential monotony and simulate 'real' speech.

- Look for your own examples in Shakespeare's plays and poems and be prepared to discuss the effect of the heroic couplet when it is used as dialogue or in the sonnets.

- Find examples of where Shakespeare uses the sonnet form as dialogue in plays.

You will surely have noticed that this entry provides you and your students with some ideas for a talk with demonstration on the heroic couplet. Candidates will be unlikely to obtain credit for using the same examples but, if they gain the necessary knowledge and understanding offered here and present it in their own words with their own examples and reference to the appropriate literary terms, then they will have achieved the necessary competence for an award at Advanced level.

'All Nature is but Art, unknown to thee;
All chance, direction, which thou canst
not see;' [...]

(Alexander Pope, An Essay on Man)

IMAGINATION

Every piece included in Anthology Online is the product of someone's imagination: probably the single most important factor in all our work. When Shakespeare has the Chorus in Henry V ask the audience to work on their 'imaginary forces' he goes right to the heart of what performance entails: a fictive world is created in which the audience must believe.

The ability to make images in the mind and then to translate them into words and actions is an essential part of the creative process. Our childhood is characterised by the ability to create imaginary friends and situations; to use the most commonplace objects as toys and to play with language. In drama and speech we have a unique opportunity to contribute to the emotional growth of children through their imaginations. Preparing for an examination may not seem to be a particularly creative or imaginative

process but that is only because we overlook the role of imagination in the entire process. Firstly, the young person must be introduced to and respond to the quality of the material thus bringing him or her in touch with the imagination of the creator, secondly, his or her imagination must be employed in order to turn a passage into a performance and, thirdly, he or she must work upon the imaginations of the audience. Essential to this activity, however, is the central role of the teacher's imagination. We have constantly emphasised a creative and experimental approach to the preparation of the material for examination. That small passage of prose, verse or drama can open up an entire field of imaginative possibilities. A good teacher will always find ways of introducing and working on each piece that will fire the imagination of their students.

For oft, when on my couch I lie
In vacant or in pensive mood,
They flash upon that inward eye
Which is the bliss of solitude.

(from William Wordsworth, The Daffodils in Poems of the Imagination)

JUDGEMENT

The entire process of examining Drama and Speech involves the making of sound judgements. We have already seen that the most important initial judgements are the choice of the most appropriate grade and of the most suitable material for our candidates. We must constantly remind ourselves of the **learning outcomes** and of the importance of not entering a student for an examination at too high a level or before they are totally prepared.

However, in the minds of teachers, the judgements that can cause the most anxiety are those made by the examiner(s) of their students' work. Firstly, it is vital to stress that teachers must distinguish between assessment of their students' work and assessment of themselves.

Every examiner appreciates that students can forget what they have been constantly told or take the most bizarre initiatives in the examination room and this, in no way, reflects upon the skill or dedication of the teacher. But because examiners are now so thoroughly trained to employ the **published criteria** in making their judgements, it is foolish for teachers to try to **predict the outcome** of an examination or become indignant if the results are not what they had hoped for. The one thing that our profession ought to teach us is how to deal with disappointment: there are enough shows and stories dealing with this issue in the world of performance alone to make this obvious!

In our subject, the making of judgements may include the brutally quick decision made at an audition, the rather more reflective but fairly rapid response by an adjudicator at a festival and the much more complex process of reaching a mark in an examination. It is important to point out that examining is **not** the same as adjudicating. Festival adjudicators give an instant mark based on their immediate impression of a candidate – assessment criteria are not necessarily published so the means by which the mark is reached is not always 'transparent'. Some festivals insist that every competitor receives a certificate and, if the criterion for gaining a certificate is a mark of 65 or above, the adjudicator is confined to the use of 35 marks out of a possible 100. In the context of a festival these modes of operation may be entirely appropriate and fulfil the needs of those participating: **an examination, however, is a very different experience**.

Performance analysis and assessment

With the growth of the serious discipline of Performance Studies, the entire process of analysing a performance has been subject to scrutiny by leading scholars. One of the most remarkable of these thinkers has been Patrice Pavis, Professor of Theatre at the University of Paris. His book *Analysing*

Performance and his constant search for ways of evaluating performances in theatre, dance and film have established an entirely new level of debate in the field of assessment and criticism. Although his work is sometimes not easy reading, it is well worth exploring some of his ideas.

When examiners come to make an analysis and form judgements on the performance of our candidates, they are able to apply the criteria that have been developed by the awarding body after considerable debate. **These are often overlooked by teachers and candidates.**

Let's remind ourselves of the **four criteria that are listed in the syllabus for Acting and Speaking:**

- **Employ appropriate physical and vocal resources to engage an audience.**
- **Respond to the quality, form and content of the material being presented.**
- **Use space creatively and effectively.**
- **Adopt and sustain a role (where appropriate).**

You might like to underline what you consider to be the key words in this list. Begin with **engage** an audience. So many examination performances make little attempt to do that.

In reaching their judgements, examiners will ask themselves a series of questions as they observe and interact with candidates. The following checklists should provide you with an insight into the way in which examiners reach their decisions, based on the four major criteria. You should use these to evaluate your own students' work in progress.

Checklist for evaluating individual performances:

Prose speaking

- ❏ Did the speaker identify with the author's intention?
- ❏ Were thoughts communicated through the purposeful and expressive speaking of phrases?
- ❏ Were the speech sounds clearly defined?
- ❏ Was the voice produced at an appropriate volume and in an unrestricted manner?
- ❏ Was there an apt variety of intonation and rhythm?
- ❏ Was there a clear and inventive differentiation between narrative and dialogue?
- ❏ Was a story's shape and progression conveyed?

Poetry speaking

- ❏ Did the speaker identify with the writer's emotions, thoughts and intentions?
- ❏ Was meaningful and expressive use made of the poem's language and structure?
- ❏ Were the speech sounds clearly defined?
- ❏ Where appropriate, were characters given their vocal identities?
- ❏ Was the shape and progression of any narrative conveyed?
- ❏ Did the speaker's voice respond to the demands of the poem?

Acting

- ❏ Did the actor understand and convey the character and situation described by the play?
- ❏ Did the actor demonstrate insight and imagination?
- ❏ Was the characterisation convincingly defined?
- ❏ Were the stylistic choices apt and persuasively realised?
- ❏ Was the voice well-supported and tonally unconstricted?
- ❏ Did the actor employ apt and varied use of voice and speech?
- ❏ Did the actor employ apt and varied use of the body and space?
- ❏ Was the performance suitably projected?
- ❏ Was the performance shaped for the benefit of the audience?

Improvisation

- ❏ Was the actor able to create and live an imagined situation?
- ❏ Was concentration sustained?
- ❏ Was there continuous creative invention?
- ❏ Was there attention to detail?
- ❏ Was the work relevant to what was asked for?

Checklist for evaluating individual performances (contd):

Sight reading

- ❏ Did the reading capture the essence of the passage?
- ❏ Was there awareness of the listener?
- ❏ Was the content conveyed through phrases spoken purposefully and expressively?
- ❏ Was there a sense of control?
- ❏ Were the speech sounds clearly defined?
- ❏ Was the voice produced at an appropriate volume and in an unrestricted manner?
- ❏ Was there a response to the particular quality of the material?

Impromptu talks

- ❏ Was there some sense of mastery of the subject?
- ❏ Did the speaker show awareness of the audience?
- ❏ Was the content relevant and informative?
- ❏ Was there an attempt to interest the audience?
- ❏ Did the talk have some shape?
- ❏ Was the speaking clear and expressive?

Prepared talks

- ❏ Was the speaker at ease with and in control of their subject?
- ❏ Was there a genuine attempt to interest the audience?
- ❏ Did the talk have an effective shape?
- ❏ If non-verbal aids were employed, did they enhance the talk?
- ❏ If notes were used, were they non-intrusive?
- ❏ Was the speaking clear, varied and expressive?
- ❏ Was the content relevant and informative?

Response and discussion

- ❏ Was there an open and ready response to questions and comments?
- ❏ Were responses relevant to the questions asked?
- ❏ Was there an ability to discuss a variety of features of the material presented?
- ❏ Was there evidence of theoretical knowledge that could be demonstrated through practice?
- ❏ Was there knowledge and understanding relating to the pieces performed?
- ❏ Was there an ability to respond to the leads given?

Checklist for evaluating 'working together':

These further questions might be considered:

Choral speaking

❏ Did the choral approach suit the selected text?

❏ Was there an appropriate and effective orchestration of the spoken language?

❏ Was communication achieved through the expressive and purposeful utterance of phrases?

❏ Was the speaking clearly defined?

❏ Were the pieces sufficiently contrasted?

❏ Did the visual presentation contribute to the oral communication?

For Acting in Pairs and Groups

❏ Where appropriate, were the introductions clear and useful?

❏ Was the overall presentation organised and shaped in order to engage and continue to engage an audience?

❏ Were the characters and situations clearly established?

❏ Was there effective and appropriate interaction between the characters?

❏ Was there apt use of voice, body and physical space?

❏ Did the performers create the impression that all their vocal and physical actions stemmed from an understanding of the characters and situations rather than from learning and rehearsal?

❏ Did any improvisation show an ability to create a life through sustained imagination and creative invention in relation to any theme provided?

❏ Was there a genuine sense of ensemble playing?

❏ Were the production values (e.g. costume or staging) appropriate and effective?

Finally, but of vital importance:

❏ Were the syllabus requirements met?

Before an examiner even considers awarding a mark she/he will consult the **attainment descriptors** for the appropriate subject (these are published in the syllabus) and will consider how *every* piece of work shown fits into the categories of Distinction, Merit, Pass or Below Pass. Having decided on the category of achievement for each aspect of the examination, the examiner will then award a mark accordingly. To give you an example: keeping in mind that the categories of attainment are **Distinction 85% plus, Merit 75-84%, Pass 65-74%, Below Pass 0-64%**. Imagine that a student enters for Grade 1 in Speech and Drama and presents a short extract from a play as the first task. There are 30 marks available for this section of the examination and the examiner, having watched and listened to the work very carefully and having asked themselves all the appropriate questions, decides that the work is in the **Distinction** category. That decision is based on a thorough familiarity with the **assessment criteria** and the **attainment descriptors** and must now be reflected in the awarding of a mark. In order for that piece of work to be evaluated at Distinction level it must be awarded a mark of between 26 and 30 (i.e. 85-100%). At this stage the examiner considers, for example, if the work is *just* at Distinction level or of such sustained excellence that it would be almost impossible to imagine anything better at that grade. The mark is then awarded.

Yes, this is a complex and demanding process and makes nonsense of the assumption that examiners simply think up a mark because they 'like' something or 'didn't like the poem'! It may also help people to appreciate why time is such an important commodity for an examiner and why breaks from this demanding level of concentration are so vital.

All that has been said here should lead to the most important aspect of our teaching which must surely be to lead our students to a point where they can **make sound judgements and accept and learn from the judgements of others**.

'I do not know whether to you this seems woefully obvious or dismally complicated.'

(Michael Redgrave, *The Actor's Ways and Means*)

KABUKI

It may seem pretentious and almost perverse to include an entry for Kabuki at this point. What possible relevance can an ancient Japanese theatre form have to a modern teacher and an anthology of pieces for examination? However, you will have noticed the stress that has been placed on the idea of 'narrative' and the possibilities of non-naturalistic and traditional performance methods in the collection of material we have made. The mention of Kabuki, thought to have been introduced into Japan by the female dancer Okuni in 1603, is a reminder that there is a whole world of expressive vocabulary that Western, text-based performance has failed to explore.

The original Kabuki drama consisted of playlets interspersed with dances presented on an improvised stage. Young women having been barred from appearing on stage in Japan in 1629, the tradition was inherited by young men who, like in Shakespeare's theatre, played both male and female roles. Drawing heavily on puppetry and Noh drama, the Kabuki theatre developed its own distinct form of staging, including an elevated walkway into the auditorium and the use of an on-stage orchestra to accompany the action and narrative. Ceremonial dress, highly stylised make-up and conventionalised intonational patterns in speech all combined to create a sense of 'total theatre' performance that might last anything up to 12 hours. Very elaborate variations on the original simple form of staging have subsequently been introduced and the convention that the actors remain sitting totally still and upright at the sides or rear of the stage when not playing a scene has remained a key factor in establishing the idea of 'the stage' simply being the place where the focus of the action is at any one moment.

Kabuki is only one form of ancient theatre that is available for our consideration. Anthology Online contains translations of plays from other ancient cultures, including Ancient Greece. In this case, the performance traditions have not survived and we either have to re-create them imaginatively, using what slender evidence we can, or impose more modern approaches onto the ancient texts. The Indian sub-continent is rich with ancient texts concerning performance styles, in some cases describing and categorising non-naturalistic gestures and dance steps that enable performers to enter their roles through their senses: the Chinese theatre, with much of its roots in festival and puppets, also provides a rich source of performance ideas for modern practitioners. As teachers, we ignore these new opportunities to develop and learn from ancient practice at our peril for they have provided the starting point for much of the most innovative performance work happening today.

'Above all, it is an art and does what art always does for those who practise it with passion and devotion. It enables them to absorb experience with their whole natures, and thereby to fulfil a want which is fully satisfied neither by action nor by thought. In the end, like all true art, it enhances the desire and strengthens the capacity to live.'

(Maurice Bowra writing about ancient ritual and song, quoted in James Roose Evans, *Experimental Theatre*)

LYRIC

The word 'lyric' has two distinct, specific but related meanings in modern terminology. The meaning likely to be most familiar to our students is that of the words of song, especially in a musical. Thus, we see 'book and lyrics' by so-and-so in the publication details of a show. The writer of these lyrics will be thought of as a 'librettist' or 'lyricist'. In some ways, this specific use of the word lyric is closer to the term's original meaning of 'to be accompanied by the lyre' that is

Unfortunately, the fact that a poem is 'lyrical' has sometimes provoked the worst forms of 'voice beautiful' and stilted utterance in candidates; as if they have suddenly started to speak a foreign language. As an examiner myself, I have often been amazed that a candidate who has greeted me and chatted with me in one voice, has adopted an entirely different voice for speaking poetry. The effect has been to draw attention to the voice and not to the poem.

the more general use in describing a type of poetry. So imprecise is that second meaning felt to be that, when it is included in a syllabus, Chief Examiners are inundated with calls enquiring if such-and-such a poem 'is a lyric or a narrative'!

Think for the moment about the poem entitled *A Kiss* by Frederica Rose in the Intermediate section of Anthology Online. You don't need to know anything about the poet in order to be able to respond to and understand this poem. The way in which the words have been selected and the musical sounds have been chosen enable them to transcend the writer and, by becoming common property, take on universal significance. There are many such 'lyric' poems, some anonymous, dealing with such themes as love, grief, time, joy, sadness, life, death or immortality. The subjects are not presented as discussions; they are stated, often very simply and directly and the poems reveal the poet's feelings and private thoughts.

Speaking such poetry may be demanding because the experience of reading it silently is itself a highly rewarding and unique experience. In silent reading, the reader can come directly in touch with the voice of the poet and, if lyric poetry is spoken aloud, the listener must have the same experience. The effective speaking of lyric verse demands an appreciation of an entire poem, so that the listener experiences a totality rather than a string of pleasant sounds that have little coherence. The words of the poem may create powerful images but these must be an integrated part of the whole so that the listener can relax, focus and follow the lines of thought and feeling expressed.

In preparing a lyric poem for performance, students need to absorb the qualities of the language, listening carefully to its sounds and structures, exploring the rhyme and rhythm, finding the pauses and inflections. Only when they have totally experienced the nuances of the poem should they set about trying to speak it. The speaking of lyric poetry demands restraint, a total absence of vocal display, a sense of stillness, focus, concentration and control. The pace must be such that every idea, every thought-process, every emotion can be heard and understood by the listener. The speaker's task is to share the poem with the listener.

These comments concerning lyric poetry may, of course, be equally applied to lyrical prose. It is a good idea to discuss with students and, in fact, be honest with ourselves about what we mean by something being 'lyrical'. We may be surprised by our answers and realise that subtle shifts of meaning have influenced the way we approach our performances. When a musician states that 'this is a particularly lyrical passage' do they mean the same as we would in describing a piece of prose: if so, *what precisely* do we mean? You may wish to look carefully at the passages of prose and verse you and your students are working on and test your definitions.

'Lyrical poetry uplifts language into a fitting expression of human emotions. In learning to speak it with full conviction it would be advisable to choose first a poem expressing something you yourself have already felt. Memorise the words thoroughly and then speak them out confidently, flooding your speaking with your own recollected emotion, fused with that of the poet.'

(Betty Mulcahy, *How to Speak a Poem*)

MYTH

Myths, legends, fables, parables, allegories and fairy tales all have meaning beyond their narratives. We only have to consider the enormous popularity of *Harry Potter*, *The Lord of the Rings* or *The Chronicles of Narnia* to see the enduring power of myth. Myths offer an explanation of natural phenomena in story form. They contain archetypal situations and characters. For the great psychologist, Carl Jung, myths provided insights into aspects of the self and some of the archetypal figures he identified form the basis of the 'Sesame' method of movement and drama therapy which invariably works through enacted myths.

Myths may also explore the origins of a race or culture and, like legends, have been handed down, very often orally, for generations. They may include fabulous creatures and deities and describe feats of remarkable physical or moral strength or acts of supreme folly. Legends usually concern themselves with the deeds of figures who *may* have existed but whose lives have become embroidered in the telling. Fables and parables tell mythical stories with a simple moral, the former tend to use animals whereas the latter have a predominantly human element and include some of the plays of Brecht. An allegory is a more complex series of personifications of moral qualities but may, like myths and legends, have some basis in historical fact. Fairy tales encompass some of our deepest fears and loves within the framework of a world in which supernatural beings interact with human lives.

None of these forms of story has its basis in literal truth: they are all concerned with higher truths, deep psychological and philosophical issues and with the relationship between the physical and spiritual worlds. Accordingly, they are primarily concerned with the **imagination** and, as such, are the richest possible source of literature and performance. For this reason, Anthology Online contains many varied examples.

SUGGESTED ACTIVITIES

1. Exploring Anthology Online

Find the following pieces in the Anthology and decide which category to place them in: Myth, Legend, Fable, Parable, Allegory or Fairy tale.

The Tortoise and the Hare, The Fish of Maui, The Bogus Boo, Little Red Riding Hood, Loreley and the Sailor, Joha and his Ten Donkeys, Magic Words, The Cave that Talked, The Obstinate Hodja, Santa's Supper in Sunland, Turtle Island, Snow White, Flannan Isle, Wind in the Pylons, The Epic of Gilgamesh, The Prodigal Son, The Rainmaker, The Mahabarata, Marouf the Cobbler, Gulliver's Travels, Agamemnon, The Great Stage of the World, Everyman, Alcestis

Discuss these and find other examples.

You will notice that this imaginative material encompasses prose, poetry and drama: the material is almost interchangeable in terms of genre as the same myth or legend may provide a play, a prose passage, a poem or a piece of verse drama. Notice, for example, how *The Smuggler's Leap* started life as a local legend and then became a popular narrative poem and, finally, a play.

2. Dramatising a myth, legend or similar story

The process of turning a story into drama is relatively simple and may provide a wealth of suitable material for examination purposes. All the stories in Anthology Online could be made into drama or indeed poems. Many of the poems could also become small plays or scenes.

A working example

The Story of Zanahari

Rather than use one of the pieces in Anthology Online I am going to work through an example that has provided me with material for several dramatisations, including a small, published musical. I first encountered this story, which may be of Turkish origin, when I was part of a holiday project with a high school drama teacher in the USA. We were devising a play to be taken to a festival of children's theatre in New York.

The story in outline

A young child named Gabor (who could be a boy or a girl) has a number of brothers and sisters who will not let him/her join in their games. In despair he/she goes to Mother and says 'I'm not clever, I'm not strong or agile and I'm not good and that is why they won't play with me!' Mother replies: 'Don't cry Gabor. You must go on a journey to see Zanahari. He gives gifts of what a person deserves to everyone who asks'. Gabor enquires as to how he/she can find Zanahari and Mother explains that during the journey he/she must go through a field of sheep without allowing any to escape, through a maze without breaking any of the hedges and through an orchard without stealing any of the fruit.

Gabor falls asleep and talks in his/her sleep about the journey ahead. The brothers and sisters overhear and vow to follow.

Gabor successfully achieves all that has been asked and arrives at the place where the great Zanahari is. The brothers and sisters, however, follow but allow sheep to escape, partly destroy the maze and eat the fruit in the orchard.

When Gabor realises he/she is in the presence of Zanahari he/she explains that he/she is not strong and agile or clever or good and asks for these gifts. Zanahari questions Gabor about the journey and discovers that he/she has done everything correctly. 'So,' says Zanahari, 'you are strong and agile because you did not let the sheep escape. You are clever because you got through the maze and you are good because you did not steal my fruit. You have the gifts you are seeking already!'

When the brothers and sisters arrive they are rude and badly behaved, asking to see Zanahari and demanding the gifts they deserve. Zanahari inflicts terrible gifts on them like a 'silly little voice' or 'a very ugly face' and the brothers and sisters are about to slink off in total disgrace.

Gabor pleads for them and, in return for this kindness, is able to play with his chastened brothers and sisters happily.

N.B. This is a bare outline and the story can be embellished and developed through discussion, improvisation and experiment.

Some decisions to make

- How many brothers and sisters are there and what are their names? (Strangely enough, my American students invented names based on things to do with eggs e.g. Scrambola, Omeletta, etc!)
- What games are they playing and how can we convey that Gabor is left out?
- What age/gender is Gabor?
- What happens when Gabor goes to Mother?
- How can we convey the idea of the brothers/sisters listening to Gabor talking in his/her sleep?
- How can we create a) the field of sheep b) the maze c) the orchard ?
- How do we convey the idea of a) Gabor and b) the brothers/sisters going on their journey?
- Where, who and what is the Great Zanahari?
- What happens when the brothers/sisters arrive to see Zanahari. What gifts does he give them?
- What happens when Gabor asks for them to be forgiven?
- How does the story end and what does Mother say/think?
- Is this a play for young children or for slightly older young people to perform for young children?
- What solo, pair and group scenes can be devised?

Possible scenes and key speeches

a) Scenes

- Gabor tries to join in the games and is rejected
- Gabor alone lamenting the situation
- Gabor with Mother
- Brothers and sisters plotting and trying to find out what Gabor intends
- Gabor's journeys through the field (with gates and fence), the maze and the orchard
- Brothers and sisters in each of the above
- Gabor arrives at Zanahari's home
- Brothers and sisters arrive at Zanahari's home
- The gifts
- Resolution and return.

b) Key speeches to be written/devised

- Gabor's soliloquy about rejection
- Gabor's speech to Mother and her reply
- One of the brothers/sisters reports that Gabor has been talking to Mother
- Gabor's speech in his/her sleep with brothers/sisters listening and planning to follow
- Speeches/dialogue as Gabor enters field, maze and orchard. This might include talking sheep, methods of getting through the maze, talking trees or any number of fantastic things
- Brothers and sisters in the same situations creating havoc and boasting about it
- Gabor's approach to and explanation to Zanahari. There might be guards or other characters involved
- Zanahari's speech to Gabor
- Brothers'/sisters' rude entry and dialogue demanding gifts
- Zanahari's reward and their reaction
- Gabor's pleas for forgiveness
- Various resolution speeches.

Other considerations

- Are there extracts that can be used as solo, pair or group performance in examinations?
- Does the story have a moral? If so, what?
- Here are two lines for a possible song. Can you make a small musical play out of this story:
  Go to Zanahari, it's not so very far, he
  Will give you all the presents you deserve
  Now write the rest of the lyrics!
- What opportunities for dance does this story provide?

You could use the approach suggested here for almost any of the material in Anthology Online that we have identified as myth, legend, fairy story, parable, fable or allegory.

'A myth is a sacred story set in a time and place outside history, describing in fictional form the fundamental truths of nature and human life. Mythology gives body to the invisible and eternal factors that are always part of life but don't appear in a literal, factual story. Most of the time, when we tell a story, we couch it in purely human terms. When was the last time you talked about monsters, angels, or demons when you were describing some strongly felt experience? Myth reaches beyond the personal to express an imagery reflective of archetypal issues that shape every human life.'

(Thomas Moore, *Care of the Soul*)

NON-VERBAL COMMUNICATION

This term covers a vast spectrum of human activity from informal 'body language' at one end of the continuum to 'high art classical ballet' at the other. Communication studies have tended to take a psychological and sociological approach to the understanding of the ways in which we communicate in everyday life and to feed this understanding into the field of performance.

We employ body language in every life situation. In our oral communications we **reinforce** our meanings with gestures or **substitute** them for speech altogether. Lifestyle and fashion gurus tell us that we can appear assertive, authoritative, relaxed, formal, informal, sympathetic or seductive simply by the way we enter a room, hold our head, touch our necks or by what we choose or don't choose to wear. Equally, we may appear nervous, unsure, intimidating, tense or unhappy by similar means. A smile or frown may transform a meeting or potential relationship. The study of proxemics tells us that there is also deep social, personal and cultural significance in how near we stand or sit in relation to others and we notice if someone is tactile or fearful of physical contact.

In other words, we are constantly giving off **signs** that can be **read** by a spectator and this is the basis of what is termed 'theatre semiotics'. In any performance, the audience **reads** and creates **meanings** out of all the visual aspects of the production in a way that has come to be seen as an equal partner to the spoken text. Teachers who are interested in postmodernist ideas of criticism and semiotics will find a useful introduction in the Trinity Guildhall handbook *Thinking About Plays*[3] but at this point it is important to note some of the aspects of non-verbal communication that are relevant for an examination performance:

- How does your student enter the room and set up?
- How does your student engage with a potential listener/audience?
- Does your student look as if she/he is dressed to work, attend a party or sit at home watching TV?
- Do all your student's physical movements relate to the communication in progress or are they superfluous and potentially distracting?
- Are the non-verbal signs as powerful as the spoken text?
- In a mime situation, is the physical movement the sole and exclusive means of communication?
- What level of eye contact and facial expression is involved in your student's communications and performance?
- Are your student's non-verbal communications enhancing or detracting from any imagined dramatic situation?
- Does your student's posture draw attention to itself or is it serving the performed material?
- Are gestures and movement suggested in the stage directions fully motivated?

In recent years there have been exciting developments in what is termed 'Physical Theatre' often involving dance, circus, mime and instrument-playing skills. The boundaries of what were once thought of as the distinct

[3] see Sources and resources

arts of 'dance' and 'drama' have also become less defined. The rediscovery of ancient performance techniques and the development of new forms such as Japanese Butoh have opened new perspectives on the nature of physical performance, gesture and the relationships between movement and sound. Teachers should take every opportunity to enrich their approach by attending experimental and innovative performances from groups looking to explore such issues.

'The social self is not of course inscribed via language alone, and linguistic failure may be accompanied by a whole battery of physical mannerisms.'

(Colin Counsell, Signs of Performance)

'Faces are the basis of all human interaction.'

(Robert Winston, A Child of our Time TV programme, 2006)

ORATORY

Anthology Online contains a wonderful example of oratory: Robert Emmet's Speech from the Dock. The rolling phrases, rich vocabulary, vivid images and powerful statements of this piece are already memorable when read on the page, but their impact when spoken in their original context must have been electric. To modern students, the idea of inspiring oratory may seem very outmoded and remote, but the world is not without its great communicators and you should do everything you can to encourage students to listen to speeches and participate in debate and public address.

The origins of the teaching of our subject lie in Classical Greece and Rome, where oratory or rhetoric was a highly prized skill. Modern democracy owes much to Classical civilization: public architecture, the theory of a legislative body consisting of an upper and lower house, the concept of democracy and freedom of speech, the importance of education in the liberal arts and the concept of the 'citizen speaker' to name but a few of the ideas we have absorbed.

Oratory was promoted by such thinkers as Aristotle and Cicero in the 4th century BC, who argued that a student could use the preparation of a speech as a means of learning. Athenians experimented widely with the use of oratory in their government and appointed paid teachers to develop the rhetorical arts among citizens. Students were expected to focus on the development of 'paideia and gravitas': culture and character through their studies. They were schooled in the five canons of rhetoric:

- Inventio (Invention)
- Dispositio (Disposition)
- Elocutio (Vocal tone and Sound)
- Memoria (Memory)
- Pronunciatio (Delivery).

You might well argue that these remain the foundation of good communication skills!

Classical students were made aware that the knowledge of oratorical techniques also equipped them to be better and more critical listeners. They were expected to prepare speeches that contained reason, proof and analysis and this was achieved through a focus on:

- precepts
- models
- practice.

Again, this method of teaching and study remains valid today. The first precept was that the speaker consider the audience and then engage in critical thinking about the content and delivery of the speech. We have advocated a similar approach throughout this book. In the preparation of a piece of oratory we need to make a very judicious selection of vocabulary: all the technique in the world will not help us unless we can make the words and phrases telling and memorable. At its best, oratory can sway opinions and fix attitudes for a generation: we also have to face up to the fact that oratory may be used to promote hatred and violence.

'The power and importance of oratory have been felt and acknowledged in all ages and in all countries, but more especially is its value and influence appreciated where *constitutional government has been attained and freedom of speech is the birthright of every citizen.'*

(R F Brewer, *Voice, Speech and Gesture*)

PAUSE

In 2005, the playwright Harold Pinter was awarded the Nobel Prize for Literature, probably the most prestigious award of its kind in the world. **The Nobel Academy** said in its citation:

> In his plays he uncovers the precipice under everyday prattle and forces entry into oppression's closed rooms. Pinter restores theatre to its basic elements: an enclosed space and unpredictable dialogue, where people are at the mercy of each other and pretence crumbles.

Most actors, directors and teachers would agree that an essential part of that 'unpredictable dialogue' is Pinter's use of **pause**. Pinter, himself an actor, was reportedly influenced by listening to an earlier generation of actors with their extensive use of dramatic silence. We have seen already how effective a pause can be in oratory and, in the theatre, it can be electrifying. A pause may create tension, menace or threat, it may indicate ongoing thought or it may indicate emptiness. Just as movement must proceed from stillness, so dialogue must come from and return to silence. Pauses allow an audience to perceive and create meaning: they can create the illusion that memorised spoken words have, in fact, been thought up at that moment. A pause can indicate indecision or the failure of words, the inadequacy of language at moments in our lives or the desperate attempt to know what to say. The pause gives language rhythm and structure.

The Trinity Guildhall handbook *Speech and Drama*[4] discusses pausing and most teachers are familiar with the various categories of pause used in speaking. I sometimes wonder just how useful this information is without

a real sense of awareness on the part of the speaker/performer. It is right to know technical terms provided that this knowledge is accompanied by understanding. This seems particularly to be the case with pauses because they create phrases and profoundly reinforce other means of expression. Pauses are, in themselves, a form of non-verbal communication and **most candidates for examination have hardly begun to explore what they can achieve through pausing.**

Some of the finest advice and helpful concepts on the use of pauses in poetry are contained in ***Performing Literature*** by Beverley Whitaker Long and Mary Francis Hopkins. The following short paragraph is particularly illuminating:

> The shape of poems is especially important because the basic unit of poetry is the line – not, as in prose, a sentence of paragraph. Denise Levertov says, 'I regard the end of a line, the line break, as roughly equivalent to half a comma, but what that pause is doing is recording non-syntactic hesitations, or waitings, that occur in the thinking-feeling process.' We miss the thinking-feeling process in many poems if we fail to give that slight hesitation, or break at the end of the line. Note that no drop in pitch can occur to signify falsely that the thought is ended. Instead, the hesitation is only a slight interruption.

When we apply this understanding to plays we find that the specific stage direction for a 'pause' is a relatively new invention. For most play texts we are left to our own devices but, in the 20th century, playwrights began to make their intentions for the script much clearer and more specific. For example, in his short one-act play *The Man with the Flower in His Mouth* the playwright Luigi Pirandello gives his main character no fewer than 24 instructions to 'pause'.

However, we now tend to associate the use of pauses and silence with the type of play that has come to be known as the Theatre of the Absurd. Eugène Ionesco's 1954 play ***Amadee*** contains this sequence of stage directions:

[4] see Sources and resources

MADELINE: Sit down and eat. What are you waiting for?

AMEDEE: [*sitting down next to Madeline, but facing the audience*] He may have forgiven us, I believe he has.

[*A long heavy silence; they are eating their plums*]

Ah, if only we could be sure he'd forgiven us!

[*Another silence*]

The effect of these two silences, punctuated by the dialogue (notice it is not the other way round!) is quite extraordinary in the theatre and conveys that sense of uncertainty and the impossibility of knowing the absolute truth that permeates Ionesco's plays.

In Fernando Arrabal's **The Two Executioners** that dates from a similar period we find this line:

MAURICE: But ... [*Pause*] Daddy ...

[*Silence*]

Here, the playwright is being even more specific. He may be using each of the dots to represent a 'beat'. In some American plays it is quite common for the stage directions to say 'A beat' meaning a single unit of silence. Harold Pinter has been notorious for insisting on the observance of the exact number of units of pause he wanted and, as you see here, there is a perceived difference between a 'pause' and 'silence'. The play *Promenade* by Maria Irene Fornes from which there is an extract in Anthology Online, contains several speeches that are punctuated regularly by laughter and many speeches in which beats of silence are indicated. Far too many students think of their pieces as a mass of words rather than thinking about how these words are framed by silence or by non-verbal forms of sound. If you want to emphasise a word or phrase, surround it with silence and it will become compelling.

'There is still another, and even more telling manner in which words and phrases may be made to stand out from their context, and that is by making effective use of pause.'

(Kathleen Rich, *The Art of Speech*)

'I've had two full-length plays produced in London. The first ran for a week and the second ran a year. Of course, there are differences between the two plays. In **The Birthday Party** I employed a certain amount of dashes in the text, between phrases. In **The Caretaker** I cut out the dashes and used dots instead.'

(Harold Pinter, *Writing for the Theatre*)

QUESTIONING

In a recent television programme, the distinguished paediatrician and neuro-scientist Robert Winston said 'If you want someone to be creative, try asking them questions and don't crush their replies'. Unfortunately, this very positive view of the role of questions has not always extended to the world of Drama and Speech examinations, especially as regards to the attitudes of some teachers and candidates. Examiners are now carefully trained and moderated in order to maximise the value and effectiveness of their questions, and syllabuses are sufficiently 'transparent' to ensure that there can be little doubt as to the nature of questions posed by examiners.

Firstly, let's dispel some of the more common myths about questions asked in graded examinations:

I lost marks because it wasn't the answer she/he was looking for

*Examiners **never** deduct marks, they only award them. Examiners **never** have a particular answer in mind: they simply listen to the reply and award marks according to the quality of the answer given!*

She/he didn't ask me any theory questions

*This is **most** unlikely. An examiner may ask questions at any stage in a practical exam. Just because there is not a clutch of questions asked together it does not mean that those marks for understanding and knowledge have not been awarded.*

This was a trick question

The last thing any examiner tries or wants to do is to trick the candidate. The question may not have been what was anticipated. That does not make it a 'trick'.

That question was not in the syllabus

The syllabus now clearly states what technical issues may be discussed at each grade. However, a candidate may be asked anything relevant to the performance of the piece they have presented. For example, if a candidate presents an extract from a 'period play' they might be asked about costume even if it does not specify 'costume' in the syllabus.

The examiner asked me about my performance because she/he didn't like it

On the contrary: examiners want to give every opportunity for candidates to justify what they do and to demonstrate their understanding.

We can now look at an imaginary situation for some guidance. Imagine that you have entered a candidate for Grade 3 in Speech and Drama or Performing Text and that you have prepared them to perform *Loreley and the Sailor* from Anthology Online as a 'prose passage performed from memory'. Here are some questions that might be asked and some possible answers that would score highly in the 'discussion' section. Please note that these are not intended to be 'model answers'.

Q: Can you show me how you used pauses to help you to make this piece effective in the first two lines?

A: There has always been a lot of singing on my banks [*pause*] and the most beautiful singing [*small pause*] comes from my daughter, [*pause*] the water nymph, [*pause*] Lorely. She looks and sounds so wonderful [*pause*] that nobody can resist her.'

Q: Thank you, can you now show me how you helped your performance with emphasis in the same two lines?

A: Yes, it was like this: 'There has *always* been a lot of *singing* on my banks and the most *beautiful* singing come from my daughter,

the water-nymph, *Loreley*. She looks and sounds so *wonderful* that *nobody* can resist her'.

Q: Thank you. How do you think this story came to be told?

A: It explains why so many ships were wrecked on that part of the river.

Q: Which river?

A: The river Rhine … in Germany.

Q: And is there a reason why this story is so well known in Germany?

A: Yes, there's a famous song about it.

Q: Do you know that song or could you sing it to me? Don't worry if you can't!

A: No, but I've heard a recording of it.

Q: Why is that spot on the river so dangerous?

A: There's a very sharp bend and a fast current: and a rock that juts out.

Q: Do you know anything about the place now?

A: Yes, there's a small town there on both sides of the river named after Goar.

Q: Well I won't ask you to pronounce the German name! So this piece is called a 'saga'. What's a saga?

A: It's a story that has been passed down for years: it probably wasn't written down and it's a kind of legend: Loreley wasn't a real person but stories grew up about her.

Q: Thank you for answering the questions. I hope perhaps that, one day, you will be able to see the Loreley rock for yourself.

'There are marks floating around all over the room just waiting for you to pick them up!'

(Professor David Male preparing student teachers for a drama viva)

RECITATION

This term has been used both as a noun and a verb. A 'recitation' may be an event or an act. We tend to treat the word 'recite' with some suspicion nowadays. The recitation of a piece may suggest a passage of memorised and often spoken prose like a creed, where, perhaps, the words are 'recited' with little conscious thought as to their meaning. We also, perhaps, think of a rather formal treatment of spoken poetry.

But this was not always the case: in fact, precisely the opposite was true of one famous set of 'recitations' which provided much of the basis of what we now refer to as 'Speech and Drama'. We shall consider this piece of our history shortly.

In the 19th century it was quite common for famous or aspiring actors and actresses to hire a public hall for the purpose of giving a recitation. Some evidence of these events has been preserved in old published collections of favourite recitation pieces, in illustrations and even in the very early examples of sound recording. Actors and actresses would hold audiences spellbound by what we would now call a 'platform performance' or 'recital' in which they would perform prose, poetry and drama, probably wearing formal 'evening dress' and relying entirely upon their elocutionary skills. However, this style of verse speaking began to strike some critics as very exaggerated and stilted.

In 1912 movements began in England and Scotland to encourage good poetry speaking through competitions and when the poet John Masefield was asked to adjudicate one such competition in Edinburgh, he was so impressed by the event and by the beauty of the Scottish accents he heard, he was determined to establish his own event in Oxford and to involve leading poets of his day, such as W B Yeats, Walter de la Mare and Gilbert Murray (whose translation of *Alcestis* is included in Anthology Online).

The Oxford Recitations, as they became known, were held at the University of Oxford every year from 1923 to 1929 and were part of Masefield's conviction that poetry should be communicated through the living voice and not by the printed page. He, along with the pioneer teacher, Elsie Fogerty was also determined to rescue poetry from the stranglehold of elocution which often resorted to mannered gestures and mime rather than finding the voice of the poet.

Some years ago I was watching a distinguished director working on a scene from one of the medieval Mystery Plays, of which there are several examples in Anthology Online. At one stage in the rehearsal he said to an actor 'Do less, you are trying to do too much, don't do so much acting!' Although this may strike you as an outrageous request, I have often felt exactly the same about 'exam-room performances'. I do not refer here to the apparently English characteristic of understatement, although if that is a factor in the material being presented it ought to be recognised; I am referring to a lack of faith in the material chosen that leads to exaggeration and artificial vocal gymnastics. This is precisely what Shakespeare must have had in mind when Hamlet advises the players to 'use all gently'.

We can still learn something from Masefield's experience. The great playwright George Bernard Shaw refused the invitation to adjudicate because he disapproved of the competitive element and because he believed that it was impossible to reduce an artistic performance to marks. This, of course, was long before the days of published assessment criteria and learning outcomes – you may wish to continue the debate!

Masefield was almost overwhelmed by the initial entry of over 500 competitors and the preliminary rounds were a revelation to him of the low standards that were common: 'some ranted, some acted, some flung themselves prostrate or struck attitudes' he wrote. However, he did encounter some beautiful work and his aim 'to encourage the beautiful speaking of poetry' was realised in many of the final nights of the annual event: audiences discovering the sheer pleasure of hearing poetry well spoken.

Although Masefield's 'Recitations' did not last for many years he had, in fact, laid the foundations of what we now recognise as the Festival movement and for examinations in aspects of Drama and Speech. Prior to his work the idea of awarding a mark for such a performance was virtually unknown.

'Oh, if only Yeats could hear this ... I had heard no speech so beautiful ... I could not sleep for three nights.'

(John Masefield, writing in 1922 after hearing Jean Downs from Glasgow speaking poetry)

SONNET

Verse speakers tend to think of the 154 sonnets written by Shakespeare rather as pianists regard the *48 Preludes and Fugues* by Bach: they somehow both present the ultimate challenge and almost define the requirements of the performance art itself. It is somehow inconceivable that an advanced verse speaker would **not** at some time wish to include a Shakespeare sonnet in a programme and it is significant that when the Royal Academy of Dramatic Art (RADA) wanted to produce a recording by many of its most distinguished and famous former students they elected to use Shakespeare's sonnets as the basis.

Shakespeare did not invent the sonnet and was by no means the only poet to employ this form. The sonnet, a poem of 14 iambic pentameters, was originally perfected in Italy by Petrarch (who died in 1374) and was only introduced into the English language in the 16th century by Sir Thomas Wyatt. The **Petrarchan** or **Italian** sonnet consists of an 'octave' of eight lines, rhyming ABBAABBA followed by a 'sestet', of six lines where a variety of rhyme schemes may be found. The most orthodox **Petrarchan** sonnet form either has two 'tersets' of three lines each rhyming CDECDE, as in John Milton's wonderful *On His Blindness* **or** three pairs of lines rhyming CDCDCD, as in Wordsworth's memorable *Upon Westminster Bridge*.

The **Shakespearean** or **Elizabethan** sonnet usually has three 'quatrains' with the rhyme-scheme ABAB, CDCD, EFEF rounded off by a couplet GG. Its exponents during the 16th and early 17th centuries included Richard

Barnfield, Thomas Bastard, Nicholas Breton, Henry Constable, Samuel Daniel, Sir John Davies, Michael Drayton, Fulke Greville, George Peele, Sir Walter Raleigh, William Percy, Edmund Spenser and Sir Philip Sidney. This very substantial body of work provides a rich source for performers. Shakespeare's sonnets have been the focus of years of scholarship and speculation. With their themes of mutability, time, loss, love and the immortality of authors through their works they have challenged performers by their personal intensity and refined form, and intrigued scholars as to the identity of the person or persons to whom they are addressed. For a particularly stimulating and bold view of their intent you may wish to read A D Wraight's *The Story that the Sonnets Tell*[5].

Keats used both the **Petrarchan** and **Shakespearean** form, and Gerald Manley Hopkins experimented widely with the sonnet. However, what use is all this information today, and why do we approach the speaking of sonnets with such trepidation and the conviction that they are very 'difficult'?

We must recognise that a sonnet takes roughly a minute to speak. There is a piece of ancient wisdom that says that this is the time it takes for the blood to circulate the body and that the sonnet has that sense of completeness. This is not, of course, an absolute rule and you would help your students considerably if you were to insist that, as an exercise, they take at least two minutes to speak a sonnet. The sonnet is certainly a minutely detailed and condensed set of ideas and is very often dense with highly complex imagery. Every detail must be carefully observed and shaped with a delicacy that demands great subtlety. In the **Petrarchan** sonnet the climax or key thought often comes in the final line of the first octave whereas in the **Shakespearean** sonnet the final couplet has an almost epigrammatic sense of conclusion and resolution. The convention of both sonnet forms is that they begin with outlining a problem or issue and conclude by reflecting upon and providing a possible solution or resolution to the

[5] see Sources and resources

issue. Since there is unlikely to be a complex resolution in so short a poem, the final statement may well be ironic or paradoxical but there is invariably a sense that the writer and speaker have arrived at a point of understanding that they did not have at the outset. In the **Petrarchan** sonnet the progress towards understanding is more gradual: the first eight lines presenting the problem or issue and the final six lines working towards a completion or resolution.

SUGGESTED ACTIVITY

The purpose of developing an understanding of the sonnet is partly that the form is very much alive and well today. We might reinforce our understanding by looking closely at a sonnet by a poet whose work is featured in Anthology Online, Winifred Mustoe. Here is her sonnet **Winter Morning**[6]:

Softly this moment of perception shakes
The spirit's heavy veil of apathy.
To sudden glimpse of larger destiny
A deeply-slumbering mid-winter wakes.
Now skies are clear, the frozen black earth breaks
Into a foam of blossom. Every tree
Rustles its new-born leaves in revelry
To match the eager song a blackbird makes.

Slowly this moment or perception dies.
Frosted the boughs, the earth still dark and bare.
No flower flaunts its beauty in the field.
No bird entreats with song the heavy skies,
Yet something indefinable and fair
Betrays the life in seeming death concealed.

Now answer the below questions.

- Why might a modern English poet select the Petrarchan form?
- There is often a substantial pause between the octave and sestet. Is this the case in this poem?
- How does the sestet resolve the issues raised in the octave?
- Although there is no final couplet, does this poem have an equivalent?

- What deeply personal idea is embedded in the poem?
- How would you handle the enjambed lines in the performance of this poem?
- What problems for breath control are posed by this poem?
- At what level would you expect a student to comprehend fully and appreciate this poem?
- How long does it take to perform?

'In any case, it is not the anthologist's task to provide the lazy reader with literature in capsule form – 'swallow this and there's no need to bother any more' – Instead, it is his job to encourage the reader to go on searching ...'

(Edward Lucie-Smith in the introduction to *The Penguin Book of Elizabethan Verse*)

TEXT

Anthology Online brings together some of the world's great texts, as well as many new and challenging pieces. Access to great texts is part of every young person's birthright and we regard text as a sign of civilization. The fact that there is also a syllabus strand entitled 'Performing Text' indicates the importance that Trinity Guildhall attaches to engaging with written texts of high quality.

The process by which a text becomes a performance is complex and will vary considerably according to the nature of the text and the performer. Anthology Online contains several examples of texts that originated in one form but have been transformed for the purposes of performance. Nevertheless, we should always begin our exploration of a text by asking what sort of text it is: is it dialogue for a play, a novel, a personal lyric poem or a narrative of some kind? and so on. Only when we have made this initial decision can we proceed to more searching questions: for example, what is its genre, its tone, its precise form?

The difference between performing a poem, a play or a prose extract is very considerable. We may, for example, be concerned to create

6 from *Landscapes* by Winifred Mustoe, see Sources and resources

a 'character' or we may want to be the 'voice of the poet' or we may wish to be several voices. We may equally wish simply to enable an audience to hear and digest the words of a poem as if we are a medium making this possible but remaining detached from the process.

In general, examiners find that there is **too much technique and too little text** in the approaches of candidates to chosen pieces. In other words, there is frequently far too little close scrutiny and careful work on the texts themselves. Most candidates would achieve far better results with intense concentration on the precise words and shape of the text. There should be few questions about the text that they cannot answer.

The traditional view of the text was that, by close study, the 'meaning' could be discovered and communicated in performance. There is absolutely no reason why you should not continue to use a text in this way, but you should be aware of relatively new approaches that are outlined in the Trinity Guildhall handbook *Thinking About Plays*[7]. Another result of the collection of ideas that we label 'Postmodernism' is that the 'text' is regarded by Performance Studies students as something that emerges in rehearsal and includes such elements as physical movement or lighting. So, in their terms, a 'text' is made from the original 'work'. This has led to some notable disputes between writers and performers: the former objecting to the liberties being taken with their texts. In Trinity Guildhall examinations there are opportunities for the creation of texts in the devised aspects of group performance and performance arts but, where the examination demands the use of a published text, you should consider it a minimum requirement to preserve that text with accuracy, care and integrity.

'The meaning of a work of art is not exhausted by, or even equivalent to, its intention. As a system of values it leads an independent life.'

(Rene Welleck and Austin Warren, *Theory of Literature*)

UNDERSTATEMENT

If you look at many of the texts in Anthology Online, you will find that they demand a direct simplicity of performance. Even the most deeply emotional or fast-moving passages of action have sufficient quality for the performer to employ subtle changes of pace, pitch, volume and emphasis and, above all, to explore the potential of pausing. If the audience is able to follow the thought-lines of the writer and to enter imaginatively and wholeheartedly into a fictional situation, the performance has achieved something remarkable. Far too often the audience is simply aware of technique and has no time to 'process' the material being thrown at them.

As an exercise, take any of the Medieval speeches from Anthology Online and experiment with how simply you can speak the lines and register the feelings. Try to remember that sensation as you approach more complex, but no less profound, passages.

'Now, anything so overdone … is from the purpose of playing.'

(William Shakespeare, *Hamlet*)

VOICE

The problem with voice has often been that it has been thought of as a static subject. Some teachers take the line 'I know about voice and what I know, I know!' In fact, since the pioneering work on the voice undertaken at the start of the 20th century, the understanding and knowledge available on this subject has increased almost daily. That is why it is so difficult to recommend a standard textbook: today's most celebrated book may become tomorrow's out-of-date 'has been'. So where are we to go for information and help and what should we be teaching?

There are three major developments in attitude and understanding that provide us with clues as to the best ways forward:

- The vocal instrument is not confined to a small area above the waist: it operates within the entire body.

[7] see Sources and resources

- Knowledge of the structure and function of the mechanisms of voice may not help us artistically but enable us to **care for the voice.**
- We must recognise when we are using textual material simply for vocal exercise and **not confuse this with oral interpretation.**

The implications of these three points are tremendous. For example: the first point reminds us that breath, health, posture, fatigue, relaxation, movement, exercise, mental well-being, self-image, attitudes, culture, legs, arms, waists, torsos, shoulders, feet, toes, fingers, chests, spines, bones of all kinds and dress **all** impact on our voices and that is **before we have considered our environment.** The sheer inadequacy of learning a bit about the 'vocal cords' becomes obvious.

Organisations, such as the 'Voice Care Network' and many of the vocal workshops conducted at such venues as The Centre for Performance Research in Wales, remind us of the rapidly developing fields of vocal studies and the help that is widely available if we look beyond the confines of traditional 'Speech and Drama' tuition and its attendant textbooks. Voice International, who organise an International Festival of Voice, produces fascinating insights into ways of working with the voice from the approaches of Kristin Linklater to that of practitioners from Poland, Ukraine and Senegal.
www.voiceinternational.org.uk

'*The voice has to be balanced with articulation.*'

(John Miles-Brown, *Directing Drama*)

WORKSHOP

We can use the term **workshop** to describe a place, an event or an activity but, in each case, the word implies the **making** of drama through practical work and experiment. The idea of a workshop or 'workshopping' has also become a means for the study and exploration of Drama and Speech and many of the issues we have encountered in this book may well benefit from such an approach.

The term workshop has become almost synonymous with the concept of a laboratory: a term also suggesting investigation and experiment.

We tend to associate the idea of a workshop with the approach employed by the English Theatre Director Joan Littlewood at Stratford, East London, in the middle years of the last century. At her famous **Theatre Workshop**, works by unknown playwrights were given a stage life and her legacy included such plays as *A Taste of Honey* and *Oh! What a Lovely War*.

The **laboratory** concept owes a good deal to Peter Brook and Jerzy Grotowski, but we can also see the influence of Bertolt Brecht and other experimental practitioners in dispensing with the conventions of playwriting and directed rehearsal by creating pieces of theatre through improvisation and exploration. What we now term 'devising' is a product of such activity.

Teachers can easily create their own drama workshop as a means of investigation and preparation for examinations, provided there is access to a virtually empty room equipped with some chairs, stage blocks or rostra. But even most of these simple requirements can be dispensed with if the approach and attitude are appropriate. Just find an empty space and prepare for work!

Traditionally, directors and playwrights have used workshops to:

- shape material before finally creating a script
- investigate the qualities of existing texts
- find the best and most appropriate styles and methods of performance
- explore the inner life of characters through improvisation
- create community performances using primary sources and local talent.

Teachers can use similar methods to enable their students to:

- find the action embedded in the text of a play
- understand levels of text and sub-text
- explore the problems and challenges facing the various characters
- experiment with the patterns and characteristics of language
- understand the goals, motivations and ambitions of the characters
- work with the conventions of the play
- create group or solo performance pieces through experiment
- understand the play's context.

Remember that drama is an activity, not a text to be read and learned. Teachers must be prepared to assist their students to find answers rather than provide their own answers that they then impose on their students. The workshop approach is one of mutual exploration and the teacher's role may be to act as guide or facilitator.

Creating a drama workshop will involve you establishing an atmosphere in which there are no right or wrong answers. As the work progresses you may need to intervene to move work forward or to ask for a time of reflection and analysis. Some teachers like to include a 'sharing and showing' activity if they have asked groups to experiment with performance material: this needs careful handling and the establishment of the convention that other people's work is respected and watched with attention.

You may find the book *Drama Improvised*, listed in the 'Sources and resources' section, particularly helpful in establishing ways of working.

Leading a workshop

- **Adopt a flexible approach to the number involved. Six is an ideal minimum.**
- **Be aware of all participants and ensure that they are working, even if that work is observation.**

- **Set time limits for various tasks.**
- **Sit in a circle and ensure an open atmosphere for discussion and reflection.**
- **Make notes on all of your discoveries and processes.**
- **Experiment with many ways of arriving at conclusions.**

Sample tasks for a workshop

- Use stage directions as a basis for exploration.
- Use games and improvisations to explore themes and ideas.
- Take very small pieces of text and play with them.
- Create new and imagined scenes between characters.
- Refine sources, such as diaries, as text.
- Work on physical aspects of performance.

SUGGESTED ACTIVITIES

You will find some suggestions for the use of a workshop approach to Shakespeare in the chapter in this book devoted to his work. At this point we are providing two examples of the way in which a play may be investigated, using contrasting plays that are introduced in Anthology Online: the 19th-century play by T W Robertson, *Caste* and the 16th-century play by Christopher Marlowe, *Dr Faustus*.

1. Exploring *Caste*

T W (Tom) Robertson was one of the first dramatists writing in English to attempt a thoroughly 'naturalistic' style of writing and was anxious to encourage settings and acting that reflected that idea. His play *Caste* is set partly in the world of the 19th-century theatre, and we must remember that women who worked as performers at that time had very low social esteem. When the world of these performers rubs shoulders with the world of social aristocrats there is an immediate cause for tension.

Quite early in Act I of the play we see a meeting between the Hon. George D'Alroy (his name suggests privilege), Captain Hawtree (another aristocrat) and the two sisters Esther and Polly Eccles, both of whom work in the theatre as actresses and entertainers. One of the play's major themes is status and the problems associated with love affairs between two people of different status. The action takes place just after a rehearsal: George has come to introduce his friend Hawtree to the two women.

Try the following

- Using the stage directions from the opening of the play, imagine you are an estate agent, showing the rest of your group around the stage setting.

- Read some of the dialogue from Polly and Esther, then create an imaginary scene in which both of them are involved in a rehearsal with the Stage Manager. Remember that in 19th-century theatre the Stage Manager ran the rehearsals.

- Take the following short section of dialogue and work on it in pairs, noticing particularly the use of the convention we call 'an aside'.

  GEORGE: [*flurried at the sight of her*] Good morning. I got here before you, you see.

  ESTHER: Good morning. [*sees HAWTREE – slight pause, in which HAWTREE has removed his hat*]

  GEORGE: I've taken the liberty – I hope you won't be too angry – of asking you to let me present a friend of mine to you: Miss Eccles – Captain Hawtree. [*HAWTREE bows. GEORGE assists ESTHER in taking off bonnet and shawl*]

  HAWTREE: [*back L. aside*] Pretty.

  ESTHER: [*aside*] Thinks too much of himself.

  Use the stage directions to tell you what is going on physically in the scene. Notice that the staging envisaged is 'end-staging' or 'proscenium arch' so that the term 'L' implies the left of the stage looking out towards the audience.

- The introduction of Captain Hawtree by George is very formal and very different from how we might introduce a friend today. Work on this moment, trying to imaginatively recreate the original manners.

- The status game: This is a way of exploring the ideas of status in the play

  One person is a master or mistress and the other a servant. The master or mistress calls the servant for a 'telling off' but the servant looks away intermittently. Whenever the servant looks away, he/she makes a rude gesture: when this happens and the master or mistress notice, they hit their servant over the head with a balloon or rolled-up newspaper and continue the dressing down. Then the servant behaves similarly to another servant and the two play with ideas of status in an attempt to exchange low status for high status.

- Improvise a discussion in which Polly and Esther talk about the two men.

- Although Polly has not arrived in the tiny extract provided, imagine her arrival after a very hard day's rehearsal. How might she react to the male presence?

- As the play progresses, the idea of a relationship between the aristocratic men and the actresses from a lower social class becomes a central issue: improvise scenes in which the men seek to justify themselves to their strict parents.

- Create a contemporary equivalent to the problem mentioned in the previous point and act it out in various ways.

- Devise a 'soap opera' based on some of the events and attitudes of the play.

2. *Dr Faustus* by Christopher Marlowe

This is one of the truly great plays of 16th-century English-speaking theatre. Written against a background of religious upheaval and debate, political uncertainty and a quest for knowledge, the play takes the legendary figure of Faust and presents his internal struggle with ideas and concepts of God, Heaven and Hell. At some points in the play, Faustus, who sells his soul to the devil in exchange for 24 years of unbridled freedom and power, hears the inner voices of his conscience, represented by two angels:

> GOOD ANGEL: Sweet Faustus, leave that execrable art.
>
> FAUSTUS: Contrition, prayer, repentance – what of these?
>
> GOOD ANGEL: O, they are means to bring thee unto heaven!
>
> EVIL ANGEL: Rather illusions, fruits of lunacy,
> That make men foolish that do use them most.
>
> GOOD ANGEL: Sweet Faustus, think of heaven and heavenly things.
>
> EVIL ANGEL: No, Faustus; think of honour and of wealth.

This passage is rich with possibilities for practical exploration. This tiny extract represents a key moment in the play and deals with some of its main themes and ideas. The passage also provides an ideal opportunity to experience the power of Marlowe's language. Remember that Faustus has been experimenting with magic and divination, hence the term 'that execrable art'.

- Find ways to make the voices of the Angels internal to Faustus.
- Place this scene in a modern setting with the same issues of internal conflict.
- Enact the scene as a dance or a movement sequence.
- Explore the ideas of temptation to power in an improvisation.
- find music or sound effects to accompany this short scene.
- use video or some other kind of moving image technology to create this scene.

You will see that the potential for investigating any play or devising any play through workshops is enormous. In the workshop situation, material and performance remain fluid and the idea of an audience only becomes relevant when experimentation gives way to preparation. Teachers would often benefit from considering the performances that eventually constitute an examination presentation to be part of 'workshop productions'.

'The company then undertook a workshop/ discussion period which included sessions with women who had special areas of expertise.'

(David Edgar describing the genesis of his play *Teendreams* with the feminist company *Monstrous Regiment* – Preface to the 1979 edition of the play)

X FACTOR

This term has come to mean 'that extra something in a performer that we cannot define'. Examiners, teachers and adjudicators all know the experience of suddenly being arrested by a performance of such dazzling quality that words seem inadequate and we jump to the conclusion that the person concerned has what it takes to be a 'star'. The history of performance is certainly peopled with characters who seemed to defy the norms of expectation: singers who have achieved enormous popularity with 'poor' voices, actors with physical limitations or strange speech who have held audiences spellbound, dancers who threw over the 'rules' of performance or whose bodies did not conform to popular conceptions of beauty or proportion: the list is endless. But is that 'extra' really beyond definition and does it help us to believe that it is?

Examinations are built on the premise that the arts we treasure are capable of analysis and the development of recognised criteria. It *is*, in fact, possible to say *why* a particular performance moves or engages us. That is why we can bring the skills of 'reading' all aspects of a performance to our judgements. When we have the thrill of recognising enormous talent, an experience we do not get too often, we are still able to evaluate the skills being used. Rather than rely on some mentally lazy assertion that a student has an unknown (X) factor, we can use the concept of an 'integration mark' or a summarising comment to indicate the way in which a performer puts his or her skills at the service of the material and audience.

'A man may act better or worse on a particular night from particular circumstances, but although the execution may not be so brilliant, the conception is the same.'

(Edmund Kean, quoted in Oscar Brockett, *History of the Theatre*)

YOUNG PEOPLE'S THEATRE

One of the most significant shifts in the location of preparation for examinations in aspects of Drama, Speech and Performance has been in the recent development of a range of young people's theatre schools. At one time, the predominant centres of teaching for grade examinations were private teachers and teachers in private primary or secondary schools. Much of this excellent work was, and still is, the result of one-to-one teaching and, consequently, the majority of examinations entered for were of a solo nature. Some teachers, working in their own studios or in the context of a school, have been able to operate with small groups and this has led to a number of 'group' examinations. However, the emphasis has been on individual skills, and production work, where it has been attempted, has more often been entered for a competitive festival, rather than examination.

In the last 20 years or so, there has been a significant change. Speech and Drama, or Creative Drama has been increasingly neglected in some parts of the education system and the creative energy of the subject has found its way into clubs and performing groups, sometimes facilitated by visiting tutors. At the same time, Drama and Theatre Studies has become an increasingly popular subject in its own right in secondary education, with major awarding bodies offering appropriate certification. State schools have also begun to make use of the awarding bodies that have traditionally offered qualifications in Drama and Speech, especially since those bodies have achieved accreditation by government departments including the QCA and similar bodies in the UK.

A further very substantial development has been the proliferation of several highly successful franchises of young people's performing arts schools operating at weekends and during holidays, combining skills in acting, singing and dancing and building on the ever-increasing popularity of Musical Theatre. Many such groups have been glad to use the opportunities for validation of their work offered by the growing number of group examinations created by such awarding bodies as Trinity Guildhall. Further encouragement for theatre for young people has come from regional and national theatres with outreach programmes, and the establishment of youth theatres by education authorities.

All these developments have had important results for teachers:

- Significant playwrights creating material for young people (a major new market for them)
- The emergence of new publishers specialising in plays and musicals for young people
- A growing emphasis on drama as a cooperative rather than a one-to-one subject
- The development of examinations in Performance Arts and Musical Theatre
- The need for performers to develop teaching skills to cater for the needs of part-time performing arts schools
- A shift in emphasis in school drama teaching, away from drama as a learning and developmental medium, towards performance and devising.

Teachers who have comfortably worked in one sector of education, be it private or state, may find these developments unnerving but our examinations and Anthology Online are designed to cater for all approaches, and the demand of the developments outlined here has produced a wealth of imaginative and attractive material from commercial publishers, teachers and writers.

'Does a children's play qualify as 'art'? Is it to be judged by these exacting standards? Theatre at any level must take into account what it gauges to be the character of its intended audience if it is to connect at all. But what distinguishes theatre for young people is the fact that it addresses itself to the immature.'

(Alan England, *Theatre for the Young*)

ZANNI

We conclude this alphabetical journey with the name of some of the most important character types in the **Commedia dell'arte** of 16th and 17th century Italy. The **zanni** were the servants, and **commedia** scripts usually required one clever and one stupid, although some involved more. The zanni were invariably part of the intrigues, and their plotting and scheming kept the plot moving at a great pace and involved either helping or thwarting their masters. Most of the **zanni** were men, although there were sometimes rather coarse and witty maids who flirted with the male servants and attracted the attention of older males.

By far the most popular of the **zanni** was Arlecchino (Harlequin), and his intrigues with Colombino (Columbine) were legendary.

If you refer to the scenes between Caliban, Trinculo and Stephano in *The Tempest* you will clearly see how Shakespeare was influenced by the **zanni**, and there is considerable evidence that the play made use of an existing improvised plot outline. In our modern performance traditions we have almost lost the clowning and improvisational skills that made the **commedia** such a popular form of entertainment, but the Trinity Guildhall syllabus encourages exploration of such techniques, partly in the performance

of pieces such as these scenes from *The Tempest* and also in the devised drama opportunities. Above all, we hope that mention of the **zanni** will encourage you and your students not to be afraid to 'make fools of yourselves' sometimes: we often take ourselves far too seriously in this profession!

'In this theatre of the actor, the accent was on mastery of the body, the art of replacing long speeches with a few gestures and choreographing the movements of the actors as a group, using space on the basis of a staging before its time.'

(Patrice Pavis, *Dictionary of the Theatre*)

7. Shakespeare the playmaker: A case study in knowledge and understanding

7. Shakespeare the playmaker:
a case study in knowledge and understanding

The plays of William Shakespeare are probably the most popular form of entertainment ever devised by a single person. Every day of the year someone in the world is preparing, performing, watching or reading about a play by Shakespeare. His plays have been translated into more languages than the work of any other writer and have been made into films, TV programmes, musicals, ballets and operas. Because Shakespeare is a universal writer and his work is enjoyed in every continent, Trinity Guildhall has a strand of the syllabus entirely devoted to his work and we have included a number of examples in Anthology Online (**www.anthologyonline.org**). We would expect many candidates to consider Shakespeare's poetry when making choices for verse speaking, and we have also included a number of his verses that have attracted composers to write settings for them.

Because so much is written about Shakespeare and his contemporaries, it is often difficult for teachers to select what knowledge and understanding is relevant for their students and candidates. A series of suggestions for the kind of information that candidates should find useful is provided below.

Comparatively little is known about the life of William Shakespeare, but we do know that he was born in the English town of Stratford-upon-Avon during the reign of Queen Elizabeth I and died there during the reign of James I. So famous is Shakespeare throughout the world that more visitors from other countries visit Stratford than any other town in Britain besides London.

The most important fact we know about Shakespeare is that he spent most of his adult life working with actors in London and that, after his death, a collection of plays bearing his name was published. There are records of performances of these plays during his lifetime but we cannot, at the moment, actually prove that he wrote them. The major problem with the authorship is that the boy Shakespeare would probably have attended the Grammar School in Stratford and learned some history, Latin and Greek but never went on to study at a university. But, whoever wrote the plays clearly had a very extensive knowledge, not only of these subjects but also of travel, life at court and politics. Strangely, Shakespeare left no books in his will, but fairly recently an inventory of a coffer (or chest) was discovered that listed a collection of books which included many identified as the likely sources of his plays. This coffer belonged to a mysterious M Le Doux, who some scholars believe to have been the code name of the university-educated playwright Christopher Marlowe who we know worked as a secret agent and who died or, some would say, 'disappeared' in suspicious circumstances. This is only one of many possible explanations for the authorship of the plays attributed to Shakespeare and, even if the man who was born in Stratford did write the plays, we can be pretty certain that there was a good deal of collaboration between playwrights.

This level of uncertainty might surprise you but you must remember that Shakespeare inhabited a world that was, in some respects, entirely unlike our own but in others, very much like ours. For example, it was a world of secrecy, torture, interrogation, power-struggles and, what we would now call terrorism. There was exploitation of poor countries by the rich and tension between followers of different forms of faith. There was an enormous demand for new plays and certainly little time to present them in a permanent written form. The plays of Shakespeare and Marlowe also dealt with dangerous issues so the fact that there may be some doubt about authorship is nothing remarkable and simply means that it is unhelpful to imagine that 'facts' about the life of William Shakespeare are necessarily helpful in understanding the plays. However, as these brief paragraphs have demonstrated, there is a good deal to be gained by understanding the political and theatrical conditions under which the plays were written.

Fortunately there are many things about this remarkable dramatist of which we can be certain. Here are some key points:

What was Shakespeare?

He was a play**wright**: that is a **maker** of plays. He seemed to know exactly what his audiences wanted: plenty of action, intrigue, romance, suspense, humour, spectacle, mistaken and disguised identities, and magic. His plays were invariably daring, new and experimental and could provoke a wide range of emotions from the spectators. Ever since Shakespeare's time, actors, actresses and many other performers like comedians and singing stars have wanted to appear in his plays and it is possible to list some of the elements that he used to make his work so successful and enduring.

The theatre itself

Most of Shakespeare's plays were written to be performed in an open-air theatre as illustrated in the Trinity Guildhall handbook *Thinking About Plays*[1]. There are now several working re-creations of such theatres, including the Globe on the site of Shakespeare's original theatre on the South Bank of the Thames in London. Some of his plays were also written for special occasions like royal weddings and would have been performed privately indoors and we know that, towards the end of his career, Shakespeare's company acquired a permanent indoor theatre.

The form and shape of theatres like 'the Swan' and 'the Globe' influenced the kind of plays that Shakespeare created: because of the large, open stage which was virtually in the centre of the audience, it was particularly

suitable for scenes in which actors shared their thoughts by talking aloud to the audience in what we call a 'soliloquy' and we have devoted several pages to examples of this in Anthology Online. Two rear entrances to the stage, however, also made this kind of theatre ideal for fast-moving action in which groups of people rushed in and out across the stage, as they did in battle or comic scenes. We know that a trap door led beneath the stage and that there was also a gallery and some sort of inner space which could be curtained off (the discovery space). Many of Shakespeare's plays contain stage directions or instructions like 'within', 'above', or 'discovered' which tell us how he used his theatre. Be sure that you realise, however, which of the stage directions in your edition of the play are 'original' and which are the work of later editors.

The permanent indoor theatres led to many new possibilities, such as scenery giving the impression of perspective and three-dimensional views. Look, for instance, at Prospero's famous speech in *The Tempest* beginning with the words 'Our revels now are ended' where you will find references to clouds, towers and palaces that were probably made visible by scenic devices.

In the outdoor theatre we know that many of the audience stood round the stage. These were the 'groundlings' who were frequently very noisy. Other much wealthier members of the audience could sit on the side of the stage and make witty remarks, as some of the characters do during a play performance in *A Midsummer Night's Dream*.

The audiences in Shakespeare's theatre were probably more like a modern soccer crowd than a modern theatre audience.

There were no actresses in the plays: all the women's parts were played by boys. We believe that, at one time, there was a tall fair boy and a shorter dark-haired boy in Shakespeare's company and that he wrote plays to exploit this particular combination. Naturally, he wrote several plays in which women disguised themselves as men.

[1] see Sources and resources

In the various recent attempts to imitate or reconstruct Shakespeare's original theatres there has been some emphasis on trying to perform the plays exactly as the playwright intended. However, every generation finds new and exciting ways of presenting these wonderful plays, very often by employing modern theatre buildings and technology.

Stories and characters

The storyline of a play is called 'the plot' and other subsidiary stories in the same play are called the 'sub-plot(s)'. Shakespeare drew his plots from a wide variety of sources, including history, mythology, recent events, romantic stories or other forms of literature. He rarely actually invented the story but used even the simplest of original ideas in the most remarkable way. He particularly seemed to be attracted by stories of misunderstanding, mistaken identity and confusion, as well as by stories of people confronted with momentous and difficult decisions.

For convenience in rehearsal and in planning performance, Shakespeare's plays are divided into sections called 'acts' and these are divided into smaller units known as 'scenes'. A 'scene' will deal with a certain section of the story and may well take place in a different location from the previous or following scene.

Shakespeare also created hundreds of memorable characters: good, evil, funny, tragic, complex and simple. Some of these characters give their names to the plays themselves: Hamlet, Macbeth, King Lear, Othello, Romeo and Juliet, King Henry V, Julius Caesar, Troilus and Cressida, for example. Other plays are named after their main characters in a descriptive way: *The Merry Wives of Windsor* or *The Merchant of Venice*.

One of Shakespeare's characters, the hard-drinking Sir John Falstaff, was very popular on his first appearance in *Henry IV Part 1* and was used again in *Henry IV Part 2* and in *The Merry Wives of Windsor*. Shakespeare also provided a memorable description of Sir John's death in *Henry V* and we can speculate as to the commercial and popular pressures that made the playwright re-use this character so many times.

The words of the plays

This is one of the aspects of Shakespeare's plays which most teachers and students feel most familiar with, especially as some of his words have become part of our everyday expression. Unfortunately, it is often forgotten that the words are one of the essential ingredients for establishing **character** and there have been too many examples of teaching and learning that have hardly considered this fact.

Shakespeare would have written out his plays by hand. There would only have been one copy of the complete play and that would have been given to the 'teller': the person who was organising the production. All the actors would have had their parts written out with a few 'cues' to show them when to move or speak. After Shakespeare's death some of the actors in the company worked together to publish all his plays, and all our modern printed editions are derived from these first versions. There were errors in those first editions which made them difficult to read, so scholars still argue about parts of some of the plays.

When you first look at a Shakespeare play on the page (we usually call it the 'text'), you will notice several features:

The text is mainly written in verse. Although Shakespeare did not invent it, he did perfect a special kind of theatre language in which there are normally ten syllables to each line. This form of language is very powerful and works on the audience's imagination in a most remarkable way. It also makes the words very memorable and they often linger on in the mind, long after the play is over. Most of this verse does not rhyme, but at special moments in plays, such as the ends of scenes, casting of spells or witty dialogue between lovers, he does use rhyme. Sometimes, as a contrast or especially when rough or humble characters are speaking, the language is almost ordinary, everyday prose.

The remarkable thing about all Shakespeare's words is that when you hear them used by a skilled performer in the theatre or in a film or TV programme, they sound perfectly natural and are easily understood.

You will also notice **stage directions**.

These are of two kinds and are there to help the actors to know what to do. We need to remind ourselves that **characters** are created largely by what they **say** and **do**.

The first kind of stage direction includes such instructions as 'Enter mariners, wet' or 'a cry within'. Some of these instructions have been added to later editions of the plays by modern enthusiasts.

The second kind of instruction is in the words themselves. When, for example, Macbeth believes he sees a dagger, he says, 'Is this a dagger which I see before me ...'. If you look at the speeches from *The Tempest* included in Anthology Online you will see just how much action is suggested and how much we learn about the characters from their actions.

Costumes

Shakespeare's plays and characters demand a huge variety of different costumes and the costume designer is a very important part of any modern production. Kings, Queens, Emperors, Soldiers, Statesmen, Jesters and Clowns, Shepherds, Merchants, Teenagers, Princes and Princesses and so on all need appropriate costumes and these may change according to where and when we live. We believe that Shakespeare himself staged his plays in predominantly contemporary costume and many modern directors still do this. Some of the plays and characters have very special costume requirements: examples include the disguises in *As You Like It* and *Twelfth Night*, Prospero's magic cloak or Caliban's gaberdine in *The Tempest* or the witches in *Macbeth* described as 'wild in their attire'. Shakespeare's plays also pose the costume designer problems of spirits, ghosts, strange monsters and eccentric human beings with unusual dress habits.

Setting and lighting

So far as we know, Shakespeare was fairly limited in what he could achieve in terms of scenic devices in his outdoor theatres but, as we have noted already, he was able to experiment with quite elaborate visual effects by the time he came to present his last plays at the Blackfriars theatre. There was also the use of some forms of artificial lighting, but as this involved flaming torches, theatres were sometimes destroyed by fire as a result.

Nowadays we can achieve almost any desired effect in the theatre and, no doubt, Shakespeare would have done the same if he were alive today.

We do know that his company had various pieces of stage equipment such as a 'grassy bank' and a table with a 'quaint devise' which made a banquet disappear.

However, he and his contemporaries largely wanted us to use our **imaginations**.

At the opening of the play *Henry V* for example, Shakespeare asks the audience to imagine horses whenever they are mentioned, yet, in England and America during the 19th century, people were not satisfied with that suggestion and built several special theatres in which real horses could appear. The results were clumsy and involved such extensive 'cutting' of the text that the plays lost much of what we now value.

Shakespeare's plays often make reference to darkness, moonlight or torchlight and we can easily recreate those effects, but Shakespeare himself relied on the use of language. This conflict between imagination and reality obviously intrigued him, because in *A Midsummer Night's Dream* he introduces an argument among some amateur actors as to how they are going to get 'moonlight' into their play. One of them suggests that they simply leave the window open and allow the moonlight in, whereas another insists that they dress an actor as 'the moon' and have him enter at the appropriate moment.

The plays often take place over long periods of time and in many different imagined places: it becomes very unwieldy and slow if 'scenery' is changed for each scene as it sometimes was in the 19th- and early 20th-century theatres. In Shakespeare's plays the stage simply **represents** a place and there have been many wonderful productions with no scenery at all. You should keep this in mind when presenting a scene for an examination. In fact, there seems to be no limit to the locations in which a Shakespearean play can be presented: castles, cathedrals, open spaces, old railway stations, warehouses, barns, gardens, canal barges, bars and theatres of every kind have been used effectively.

Fights, dancing and music

Shakespeare's plays show every aspect of human society, including its violent side. Many of his plays contain duels, street brawls, battle scenes, wrestling or other forms of hand-to-hand fighting. In a production or the performance of a single scene these all have to be very carefully rehearsed under the guidance of an expert.

Dancing is used as a means of celebration or courtship. The dancing also has to be carefully arranged by a **choreographer** who may have to research the kind of dancing that was popular in Shakespeare's time or devise a series of dances or dance steps appropriate to the style of production or performance extract. Some of the dances in the plays are described by name.

We also know from the plays themselves that other forms of music besides music for dancing were frequently used in the theatre of Shakespeare's day. The playwright often tells us what particular instruments he wants: trumpets for fanfares and royal entrances, drums for military scenes, oboes for mysterious effects or pipes for folk tunes. He often specifies 'soft music' or the sound of thunder and many plays contain songs which, as you can see from their inclusion in the Anthology, can be performed on their own.

Unfortunately, the original music for Shakespeare's plays has only survived in very small quantities and so, when we produce one of the plays or present a scene involving music, we have to decide what settings to use. We do know that in Shakespeare's time the most popular form of music was the 'lute song', usually sung by a single performer accompanied by a stringed instrument. We also know that some of the best musicians of this type were living in England at the time, so we can imagine how many of the songs would have sounded. Students of early music have discovered what some of the instruments mentioned by Shakespeare looked like and experts have reconstructed some of them in order to obtain an authentic sound. However, because Shakespeare's plays appear to be for all times, every age decides on its own music and there have been many musicians from the classical, folk, jazz and rock traditions who have created new music for productions.

What were Shakespeare's plays about?

One of the greatest fascinations of Shakespeare's plays is that they appear to have something interesting to say about every experience we might have in real life. Everyone performing or watching a play can usually find something new or remarkable. The plays seem to speak to every age and generation. Here are some of the issues tackled by the playwright:

- The problems of royalty
- Tensions between families and between parents and children
- Violence and gang warfare
- Living with conscience
- The use of power and ideas of justice and injustice
- Love, sex and relationships
- International disputes
- The problems of rival groups
- Ambition, indecision and the idea of freedom
- The problems of old age

- Political power and intrigue
- Ideas of good and evil
- The concepts of redemption
- God and the human race
- Fate, destiny and history
- Beauty, art and music
- Jealousy and revenge.

What kinds of play did Shakespeare write?

We must remember that, whatever labels we might give to a play in order to place it in a certain category, we do this for our own convenience. Shakespeare himself created plays that both appealed to popular taste and gave him satisfaction as a creative artist. The following gives some indication of the wide variety of plays he wrote.

HISTORY PLAYS

This group of plays deals with events in English history including the reign of King John, and a period from the beginning of what are known as the Wars of the Roses, to the birth of Queen Elizabeth I who was alive when Shakespeare's plays first appeared. These are action-packed plays: full of power-struggles, love affairs, battles and memorable characters. They are **not** accurate history. Shakespeare had to be extremely careful not to offend the successors of some of the Kings and Queens mentioned in the plays: he risked death or imprisonment if he appeared to slander the reigning monarch so he gives a rather biased and sometimes distorted view of history. For example, Joan of Arc has often been shown as a heroine by playwrights and patriotic French historians, but in Shakespeare she is simply a nuisance to the English armies. Some of the plays are particularly patriotic towards England and it is interesting to note that, during the Second World War, the great actor Sir Laurence Olivier made a film of Shakespeare's play *Henry V* to boost British morale. In recent years, both in the theatre and on television there have been some remarkable linked series of productions of the history plays.

PLAYS OF ANCIENT GREECE AND ROME

Shakespeare was on safer ground when he drew his plots from incidents in the 'ancient world', sometimes using them as thinly disguised commentary on contemporary events. We must remember that Shakespeare inhabited a society in which the foundations of education, science, philosophy, law, art, music and literature were to a large extent based on classical learning. Christopher Marlowe, the dramatist educated at Cambridge University, for example, would have been expected to deliver his work for both written and oral examination in Latin. We can assume, therefore, that much of Shakespeare's audience was familiar with the stories and legends of the ancient world, including much of its mythology, and we know that many of the plays by other rival playwrights and companies dealt with this material.

COMEDIES

The comedies are usually set in an indeterminate time and either in a far-off place or somewhere in Shakespeare's immediate world. They show characters in some dilemma or predicament that is eventually resolved happily and often revolve around mistaken identity or disguise. Improbable situations are created when characters find lost relatives or form loving relationships after journeys to unknown places. The dialogue is witty and fast moving, with incidents of what we would now call stand-up comedy and farce. The action is invariably very physical and may well involve singing and dancing. Some of the jokes in the text are virtually incomprehensible to a modern audience because they rely on contemporary reference, but the comic situations are as fresh as ever and the fact that there is usually a very imprecise historical setting makes them very suitable for modern production. Many of the characters are flawed but loveable: vain, foolish, tending to drink too much, some of them are clowns and others are drawn from the court and the countryside in deliberate juxtaposition. Many of the comedies deal with love and its problems and are therefore tinged with an element of madness, in which the supernatural world is sometimes involved.

TRAGEDIES

These plays are set in clearly defined periods of history and include most of Shakespeare's Roman and Greek plays. They are frequently set against a backdrop of warfare between nations and rival political factions.

Potentially noble characters become engulfed by a catastrophe that results from a reversal of fortune or a fatal error of judgement. Other characters are dragged down by the descent of the **protagonist** and events become so painful that individuals are forced to reflect on the meaning and purpose of life itself. The plays contain examples of terrible evil and malevolence, scheming, jealousy, revenge and a lack of human compassion. By their conclusion the audience is left in no doubt of the consequences of a world without moral standards.

Shakespeare seems to have intended that the process of watching these plays would be both painful and cathartic. Ideas and sentiments are expressed in the most sublime poetry but the actions are cruel and spectacularly blood-thirsty. The innocent suffer but treachery does not prosper in the end. If Shakespeare had written no other plays, his reputation as the world's greatest and most popular dramatist would probably have been established by his five best-known tragedies: *Hamlet*, *Macbeth*, *Othello*, *King Lear* and *Romeo and Juliet*.

ROMANCES, TRAGI-COMEDIES OR 'LATE PLAYS'

There are a number of plays, apparently written towards the end of the playwright's career that are less easy to categorise: *Pericles*, *The Winter's Tale*, *Cymbeline* and *The Tempest*. In some respects these plays are almost like myths or fairy tales: characters suffer shipwreck yet are miraculously saved, gods and goddesses are involved in human dramas, dead people return to life or long lost relatives are reunited. Characters undertake long physical and spiritual journeys, and

forgiveness and love triumph in a happy resolution. In these 'last plays' there is a marked emphasis on youth and the hope that young people offer for the future. The older generation has missed its opportunities and sometimes, even, made a hell on earth.

As a body of work, these plays are curious and, sometimes, convoluted: they are dreamlike and not naturalistic. They are parables or fables that operate as allegories but they are, in many senses, fantastic. They deal with both the dark and light side of the human condition and present humans as highly complex and contradictory beings who relate both to the supernatural and divine, and to powers of evil.

The danger of categories

As we have seen throughout this handbook, we only categorise works in order to assist us in understanding and studying them. Just how risky this business can be is illustrated by comparing two of Shakespeare's most popular plays: *Romeo and Juliet* and *A Midsummer Night's Dream*, both written in the same year. More films, songs, musicals, ballets and operas have been created from these two plays than any other of his plays and, in some respects, they are remarkably similar. They both start with a dilemma for the young people in the story: their parents do not approve of the girl or boy with whom they have fallen in love. In the first play, the events end in tragedy with the families realising the futility of their feud; but in the second, events resolve themselves happily, even though a father has threatened his daughter with death if she does not obey his wishes. Shakespeare himself was clearly also aware of the danger of categorising plays as he presents a comic portrait of a laboured list of play categories in the words of Polonious, a long-winded character in *Hamlet*.

Performing Shakespeare today

In one sense, Shakespeare is just like any other playwright, but many students may well feel daunted by the sheer volume and scale of his *Complete Works* and approach them with an almost absurd degree of reverence and trepidation.

In recent years many teachers and practitioners have developed varied and imaginative approaches to Shakespeare – both in terms of the plays as a whole and the individual characters within them. The following extract comes from John Binfield's **Twelfth Night: from Page to Stage**[2], the first of a splendid series of books that takes particular account of the needs of young performers and their teachers.

This book provides performance extracts suitable for male and female candidates, practical commentary on possible approaches to performing them and numerous ideas for acting exercises and workshops, two of which are reproduced here.

WORKSHOP ACTIVITIES

1. Sad true lover: Orsino, Viola-as-Cesario

Devise expressive choreographed movement to music, with the following dialogue interspersed and improvised in timing and expression. The music provides the continuity and momentum as the words irregularly come to the surface. The words from the song should be sung tunefully 'off the cuff'.

or:

Orsino and Viola speak the words, the timing improvised with background music, standing very still, turned away from each other

ORSINO: Give me ... give me

VIOLA: [*echo*] Give me ... me ... me ...

ORSINO: ... some music ...
... relieve my passion.
                    [*music cue*]
Remember me ...

VIOLA: [*echo*] Remember me ... me ...

ORSINO: I am all true lovers.
Dost thou like this tune?

VIOLA: A very echo ... echo ... where love is thron'd ...

ORSINO: Thy eye hath stay'd ...
What kind of woman?

VIOLA: Of your complexion.

ORSINO: Our fancies ... giddy ... wavering.
Come, the song.
Spinsters and knitters ...

VIOLA: ... in the sun ...

ORSINO: Do chant it.

ORSINO AND VIOLA: [*sing*] Come away ...
come away ... fly away ... fly away.

ORSINO: [*sings*] Death ...

VIOLA: [*sings*] Death ...

ORSINO AND VIOLA: [*sing*] Not a Flower ...
not a flower ... not ...

ORSINO: My grave ...

VIOLA: Weep there ...

ORSINO: Tell her my love ... tell her ...

VIOLA: She cannot love you ...
You cannot love her ...
You cannot love her ...
You cannot love her ...

ORSINO: So strong a passion ...
Hungry as the sea ...

VIOLA: My father had a daughter lov'd.

ORSINO: Died thy sister?

VIOLA: Never told ... pin'd ... pin'd

ORSINO: Died thy sister?

VIOLA: Green ... yellow ... melancholy.

ORSINO: Mel ... an ... choly.

VIOLA: Patience on a monument
smiling at grief. [*music stops*]

ORSINO: Died thy sister?

VIOLA: I know not.
Shall I to this lady?

ORSINO: ... to her in haste ... tell her ...
tell her ...

ORSINO AND VIOLA: [*sing*] Come away,
come away ... sad true lover ...

Viola: To weep there ...

[2] see Sources and resources

2. Come hither, boy: Orsino, Viola-as-Cesario

Devise an improvisation for two male performers who are to play the roles of Orsino and Viola disguised as Cesario.

They are wearing contemporary clothes and both have appropriate items of Elizabethan costume laid out on a table in front of them. They begin to put on their costumes. As they do so they chat awkwardly and jokingly about love, about boys playing girls, about girls pretending to be boys and about being in an all-male cast.

Next they decide to practise before going to the rehearsal. They know their lines and begin Act 2, Scene 4 at line 8, 'Come hither, boy ...' and get as far as line 22, 'Too old, by heaven', but cannot resist the giggles and the temptation to 'send it up'.

Finally they force themselves to try again, this time from line 72, 'There is no woman's sides'. Initially, Orsino proclaims the words and Viola is self-conscious. Then they begin to connect vocally and in looks and gesture. Their imaginations take hold of the intimate scene very persuasively. They stop at line 100, on 'and yet I know not', momentarily surprised and moved by the quiet spell they have cast.

Invent some out-of-role exit lines.

8. Sources and resources

8. Sources and resources

Lists of recommended books and materials can be frustrating to compile and use because publications can so quickly become unavailable and out-of-date. However, the lists offered here have been deliberately selected to minimise this problem. Books listed are either very recent publications or are new editions of established works that are likely to remain easily available in the near future. The editions cited should be obtainable anywhere in English-speaking countries.

Trinity Guildhall handbooks

Trinity Guildhall has produced a series of handbooks especially written to help in the task of preparing students for examinations. The following will be of particular assistance to teachers working in the field of Speech and Drama:

Acting Shakespeare by Frank Barrie

Speech and Drama by Ann Jones and Robert Cheeseman

Thinking about Plays by Ken Pickering and Giles Auckland-Lewis

These handbooks and others in the same series are kept up to date to reflect recent developments. They are obtainable by mail order direct from the publisher Dramatic Lines on: +44 (0)20 8296 9502, or its UK Freephone orderline: 0800 542 9570 or via the website www.dramaticlines.co.uk

Seven Essential Texts

The following books are either seminal texts for our subject or invaluable reference books:

Child Drama by Peter Slade
(London, Hodder and Stoughton, 1980)
Remains probably the most influential and illuminating book on working with young people.

An Actor Prepares by Konstantin Stanisalvski
(London, Methuen, 1988)
One of several remarkable texts by this pioneer of actor-training that have shaped the approaches to performance in the English-speaking theatre.

Freeing the Natural Voice by Kristin Linklater
(NY, Quite Specific Media Group, 1988)
Perhaps the most significant book on voice written in recent years.

The Empty Space by Peter Brook
(Harmondsworth, Penguin, 1972)
An essential challenge to the way we think about performance.

Experimental Theatre by James Roose-Evans
(London, Routledge, 4th edition, 1989)
An inspirational survey of recent approaches to performance.

Key Concepts in Drama and Performance by Kenneth Pickering
(Basingstoke, Palgrave Macmillan, 2005)
A comprehensive and gentle guide through the labyrinth of Drama, Speech and Performance Studies.

History of the Theatre by Oscar Brockett
(Mass. Allyn and Bacon, 8th edition, 2006)
This remarkable book continues to run into many editions. It explores the performance traditions of every part of the world.

Please note that the following books are listed as in a conventional Bibliography. They include some challenging titles as well as more practical handbooks.

Recent books on teaching

Bernardi, Philip, *Improvisation Starters* (Ohio, Betterway Books, 1985)

Cassidy, John, *Can we have Drama?* (Great Wakering, Mc Crimmon Pubs, 2004)

Fleming, Michael, *Starting Drama Teaching* (London, D. Fulton Pubs, 2002)

Hahlo, Richard and Reynolds, Peter, *Dramatic Events: How to run a successful workshop* (London, Faber and Faber, 2004)

Neelands, Jonothan, *Beginning Drama 11-14* (London, David Fulton, 2nd Edition, 2004)

Novelly, Maria C, *Theatre Games for Young Performers* (Colorado, Meriwether, 1995)

Pickering, Kenneth, *Drama Improvised: a handbook for teachers and therapists* (Colwall, J Garnet Miller, NY Theatre Arts Books, 1997)

Talboys, Graeme K, *AAARGH To ZIZZ: 135 Drama Games* (London, Dramatic Lines, 2002)

Winston, Joe and Tandy, Miles, *Beginning Drama 4-11* (London, David Fulton, 2nd Edition, 2001)

Woolland, Brian, *The Teaching of Drama in the Primary School* (London, Longmans, 1993)

Worthman, Christopher, *Just Playing the Part: Engaging Adolescents in Drama and Literacy* (NY, Teachers' College Press, 2002)

Poetry and Literature

Drabble, M and Stringer J (eds), *The Concise Companion to English Literature* (Oxford, Oxford University Press, 2000)

Gill, Richard, *Mastering English Literature* (Basingstoke, Palgrave Macmillan, 1998)

Lennard, John, *The Poetry Handbook* (Oxford: Oxford University Press, 2nd edition, 2005)

Mustoe, Winifred, *Landscapes* (Birmingham and Midland Institute, 1994)

Padel, Ruth. *52 Ways of Looking at a Poem* (London, Chatto, 2002)

Peck, John and Coyle, Martin, *A Brief History of English Literature* (Basingstoke, Palgrave Macmillan, 2002)

Roberts, Phil, *How Poetry Works* (Harmondsworth, Penguin, 2000)

Wainwright, Jenny, *Poetry: the Basics* (London, Routledge, 2004)

Theatre and Performance

Allain, Paul and Harvey, Jen, *The Routledge Companion to Theatre and Performance* (London and NY, Routledge, 2006)

Kerrigan, Sheila, *The Performer's Guide to the Collaborative Process* (Portsmouth, Heinemann, 2001)

Law, Jonathon and Pickering, David (eds), *The New Penguin Dictionary of the Theatre* (Harmondsworth, Penguin, 2001)

Mamet, David, *True and False: Heresy and Common Sense for the Actor* (New York, Random House, 1997)

Pavis, Patrice, *Analyzing Performance* (Ann Arbor, Univ. Michigan Press, 2003)

Walford, Rex and Dolley, Colin, *The One-Act Play companion: a guide to plays, playwrights and performance* (London, A and C Black, 2006)

Wraight, A D, *The Story that the Sonnets Tell* (Adam Hart Publishers, 1995)

Acting and Speaking

Allain, Paul, *The Art of Stillness* (Basingstoke, Palgrave Macmillan, 2002).

Barkworth, Peter, *About Acting* (London, Methuen, 1991)

Barton, John, *Acting Shakespeare* (London, Methuen, 1984)

Barton, Robert, *Acting on Stage and Off* (Belmont, Thomson, 4th edition, 2006)

Caputo, John, Palosaari, Jo and Pickering, Ken, *Effective Communication* (London, Dramatic Lines, 2003)

Caputo, John, Hazel, Harry, Mc Mahon, Colleen & Daniels, Deanna, *Communicating Effectively: Linking Thought and Expression* (Dubuque, Kendall Hunt, 2002)

Jones, Ellis, *Teach Yourself Acting* (London, Hodder and Stoughton, 2002)

Mulcahy, Betty, *How To Speak a Poem* (London, Autolycus Press, 1987)

Rich, Kathleen, *The Art of Speech* (London, Gresham Books, 4th edition, 1979)

Other sources cited in this book

Counsell, Colin, *Signs of Performance: An Introduction to Twentieth-Century Theatre* (London, Routledge, 1996)

Cordner, Michael and Clayton, Ronald eds, *Four Restoration Marriage Plays* (Oxford, OUP, 1995)

England, Alan, *Theatre for the Young* (Basingstoke, Macmillan, 1990)

Findlay, Kirsty N and Pickering, Ken, *Preparing for your Diploma in Drama and Speech* (Twickenham, Dramatic Lines, 2nd edition with additional material by John Gardyne, 2007)

Hinton, Michael, *The 100-Minute Bible* (Canterbury, The 100 Minute Press, 2005)

Jayyusi, Salma Khadra and Allen, Roger (eds), *Modern Arabic Drama: An Anthology* (Bloomington, Indiana U.P., 1995)

Miles-Brown, John, *Directing Drama* (London, Peter Owen, 1980)

Pickering, Kenneth, *Studying Modern Drama* (Basingstoke, Palgrave Macmillan, 2003)

Taylor, John Russell, *Anger and After* (Harmondsworth, Penguin, 1962)

John Binfield's *From Page to Stage* series, which provides an approach to the interpretation, preparation and performance of Shakespeare's plays for the young performer is published and distributed worldwide by Dramatic Lines. They are obtainable by mail order direct from the publisher Dramatic Lines on:
+44 (0)20 8296 9502, or its UK Freephone orderline: 0800 542 9570
or via the website www.dramaticlines.co.uk

The Elizabethan Theater Mystery series by Edward Marston are published in the USA and Canada by St Martin's Minotaur. Details from the publisher's website www.minotaurbooks.com

9. Index

9. Index